T0289669

HBR Guide to
Managing
Flexible Work

Harvard Business Review Guides

Arm yourself with the advice you need to succeed on the job, from the most trusted brand in business. Packed with how-to essentials from leading experts, the HBR Guides provide smart answers to your most pressing work challenges.

The titles include:

HBR Guide for Women at Work

HBR Guide to Being More Productive

HBR Guide to Being a Great Boss

HBR Guide to Better Business Writing

HBR Guide to Building Your Business Case

HBR Guide to Buying a Small Business

HBR Guide to Changing Your Career

HBR Guide to Coaching Employees

HBR Guide to Collaborative Teams

HBR Guide to Data Analytics Basics for Managers

HBR Guide to Dealing with Conflict

HBR Guide to Delivering Effective Feedback

HBR Guide to Emotional Intelligence

HBR Guide to Finance Basics for Managers

HBR Guide to Flexible Work

HBR Guide to Getting the Mentoring You Need

HBR Guide to Getting the Right Job

HBR Guide to Getting the Right Work Done

HBR Guide to Leading Teams

HBR Guide to
Managing Flexible Work

HARVARD BUSINESS REVIEW PRESS

Boston, Massachusetts

HBR Press Quantity Sales Discounts

Harvard Business Review Press titles are available at significant quantity discounts when purchased in bulk for client gifts, sales promotions, and premiums. Special editions, including books with corporate logos, customized covers, and letters from the company or CEO printed in the front matter, as well as excerpts of existing books, can also be created in large quantities for special needs.

For details and discount information for both print and ebook formats, contact booksales@harvardbusiness.org, tel. 800-988-0886, or www.hbr.org/bulksales.

Copyright 2022 Harvard Business School Publishing Corporation

All rights reserved

Printed in the United States of America

1 2022

No part of this publication may be reproduced, stored in or introduced into a retrieval system, or transmitted, in any form, or by any means (electronic, mechanical, photocopying, recording, or otherwise), without the prior permission of the publisher. Requests for permission should be directed to permissions@harvardbusiness.org, or mailed to Permissions, Harvard Business School Publishing, 60 Harvard Way, Boston, Massachusetts 02163.

The web addresses referenced in this book were live and correct at the time of the book's publication but may be subject to change.

Library of Congress Cataloging-in-Publication Data

Names: Harvard Business Review Press, issuing body.
Title: HBR guide to managing flexible work.
Other titles: Harvard Business Review guide to managing flexible
    work | Harvard business review guides.
Description: Boston, Massachusetts : Harvard Business Review Press,
    [2022] | Series: Harvard business review guides | Includes index.
Identifiers: LCCN 2021058686 (print) | LCCN 2021058687 (ebook) |
    ISBN 9781647823320 (paperback) | ISBN 9781647823337 (epub)
Subjects: LCSH: Flexible work arrangements—Handbooks, manuals,
    etc. | Virtual work teams—Handbooks, manuals, etc. | Virtual
    work—Handbooks, manuals, etc. | Telecommuting—Handbooks,
    manuals, etc. | Success in business—Handbooks, manuals, etc. |
    Industrial management—Handbooks, manuals, etc.
Classification: LCC HD5109 .H37 2022 (print) | LCC HD5109
    ebook) | DDC 331.25/72—dc23/eng/20220105
LC record available at https://lccn.loc.gov/2021058686
LC ebook record available at https://lccn.loc.gov/2021058687

ISBN: 978-1-64782-332-0
eISBN: 978-1-64782-333-7

The paper used in this publication meets the requirements of the American National Standard for Permanence of Paper for Publications and Documents in Libraries and Archives Z39.48-1992.

What You'll Learn

The traditional 9-to-5 office job is no longer the norm. Individuals have the option to work anywhere, any time. The advantages of flexible work are clear: With a schedule that suits your needs, allowing you to volunteer, stay active, or take care of your loved ones, you'll be happier, more productive, and more engaged on the job. But where do you start? How do you decide what will be the best arrangement for your job and team? And what's the best way to ask your manager for it?

It's time to rethink how your work gets done. You'll have to adjust how you stay productive, communicate, and set boundaries when you're dealing with reduced hours, minimal face time with your colleagues, and an increase in online distractions. And if you're a manager leading a flexible team, you'll have to be even more intentional when it comes to creating a fair and inclusive culture and supporting people spread out across distance and time zones.

Whether you've been working on a different schedule than your colleagues for years, are hoping to find a flexible arrangement that works for you, or are managing a team with varied schedules and locations, this guide will help you navigate the challenges that arise along the way.

You'll learn how to:

- Figure out where and when you are most productive.

- Set a flexible work schedule that meets your needs.

- Negotiate a flexible work arrangement with your boss.

- Get more done—in less time.

- Help your team set a flexible working schedule.

- Stay focused when you're working remotely.

- Create an inclusive and fair environment for your team.

- Remain visible to your colleagues when you're not physically present.

- Craft communication norms for you and your team.

- Run—and participate in—successful hybrid meetings.

- Stay connected to colleagues who are online at different hours.

- Provide feedback for employees virtually.

Table of Contents

Table of Contents

Getting Started

CHAPTER 1

A Primer on True Flexibility

by Ellen Ernst Kossek, Patricia Gettings, and Kaumudi Misra

What does flexibility at work look like in practice? And how can you know whether your team or organization is using it successfully?

We are researchers who study how organizations of all types—from professional services and IT firms to hospitals, retail stores, and manufacturing facilities—manage flexibility. In the course of our work we have asked leaders how they do it (or don't). Here is a range of typical responses:

I accommodate employee needs for time to go to the gym during lunch or to take a class by allowing a special arrangement with respect to the work schedule.

Adapted from "The Future of Flexibility at Work," on hbr.org, September 28, 2021 (product #H06L8C).

If a family member is ill or someone has been in a car accident, it's no issue to leave work.

Because of the way that the units are staffed and scheduled, there doesn't seem to be a whole lot of flexibility.

I have often resorted to mandatory Zoom meetings on Friday nights at 6 p.m., because that was the only calendar opening for key staff members.

We can't get enough staff on the weekends to run the production we need to run—even with eight different schedule options. That's not a good thing. I don't want that to be the reason we can't produce.

These responses may sound familiar, and the variation among them is notable. The first focuses on special arrangements for nonwork activities. The second is contingent on dire circumstances. The third expresses frustration about the barriers to flexibility. The fourth is flexibility at its worst. The last shows that flexible scheduling is a critical (yet unsolved) competitive issue for many organizations.

This variation reflects the fact that the word "flexibility" is vague; its implementation can differ from organization to organization, department to department, and even team to team. It's no wonder that managers struggle with how to let employees work when and where they do so best. Even companies that were early leaders in piloting extensive flexible working—such as IBM and Bank of America—began pulling back on those arrangements several years ago, because they felt their businesses weren't benefiting.

Leaders have typically managed flexibility in one of two ways: as an *accommodation* around individual work-life events such as illness or childcare, which companies use to attract and retain employees, or as *boundaryless working*, which many leaders used to transition their organizations to widespread remote work during Covid-19. With the latter, employees are expected, explicitly or implicitly, to be available 24/7 to perform their jobs. Whereas accommodation largely offers flexibility for the individual, boundaryless working offers flexibility for the company. Neither is inherently bad, but both can have unintended consequences, particularly when used in isolation.

As companies move to implement hybrid flexibility— a largely employer-determined mix of remote and office work schedules, incorporating a blend of unique accommodations and widespread boundaryless work with little or no structure—employees' well-being and careers could actually suffer. We believe that women and those with health or family-care needs would be the most disadvantaged. That's because the majority of these arrangements won't effectively empower employees to align job and nonwork demands by controlling when and where they work. Our fear is that companies may end up offering *inflexible* flexibility, whereby employees have little choice about their schedules and which days they work remotely. At the other extreme, flexibility may be implemented without structures or norms, resulting in a "program" that is disorganized, scattershot, and reactive to work requirements. Expectations about where and when one should work may shift without warning, as work seeps into off-hours and employees struggle to live predictable lives outside of work.

True flexibility will require truly new thinking.

A Better Way

True flexibility aligns employers and employees to achieve mutual gain in meeting both performance and work-life needs. It is a means for companies to compete in the market over the long term, and it gives employees a say and some choice in how flexibility is implemented on their teams and in their organizations.

This is both a top-down and a bottom-up process. Leaders listen, set goals, and provide resources to make flexibility possible. Employees choose flexible working that suits their needs while communicating with their managers and colleagues to ensure that team, client, and customer requirements are met. In other words, the company provides the scaffolding—flexibility options, equipment, and supportive performance-management systems—and individual employees and teams decide how to organize their work within it.

With this approach, employers benefit by retaining a globally diverse, sustainable workforce. Employees have improved well-being, enjoy respectful team processes, and avoid burnout and health problems. But the approach requires moving away from old narratives and enhancing employee support and trust. To do that, leaders must first assess their current culture: How do they define flexibility? Has the company leaned more toward accommodation, boundaryless work, or a combination? What policies has it embraced, and for which jobs? Then they can assess which principles of true flexibility should be further embraced. We detail those principles here.

Make flexibility available to all employees

Every job deserves some flexibility. Even if telework isn't always an option, organizations should offer flexibility to both office and frontline workers; it should not be viewed as a scarce or privileged resource, yet all too often that's what happens. Companies ignore the needs of essential and hourly workers, providing flexibility only to knowledge workers on technology-driven teams.

Consider a pharmaceutical company that was part of one of our studies. During a snowstorm, senior directors and managers could work from home, but secretaries were forced to drive on a busy (and icy) freeway to get to the office. Many leaders didn't realize that they had such an unfair policy, because they were accustomed to administrative support in a hierarchical culture. The company gradually expanded its flexibility by experimenting with summer hours: A secretary could partner with a peer to cover each other's Friday workload, enabling them to take every other Friday off.

Flexibility for all workers is indeed possible. As managers learned during the Covid-19 pandemic, a company can schedule hourly work flexibly and in shorter shifts and give paid time off at the last minute without penalty; in fact, those accommodations were necessary to support essential workers during the crisis. We know of an engine manufacturer that, even before Covid-19, had highly cross-trained "floaters" who could rotate jobs and shifts on teams and fill in wherever colleagues needed help. That allowed its teams to function well during the pandemic, when workers had to care for children during school closures or take care of other personal needs. A fast food restaurant recently added paid time off and an emergency childcare program to attract mostly hourly workers. Another example comes from a busy metropolitan police department: Officers, including supervisors, were able to use predetermined compressed workweeks to create more-predictable schedules and allow for recovery time.

Increasing flexibility for frontline workers can help a company better support diversity and inclusion, because immigrants, people of color, and working mothers are heavily represented in service industries. Ultimately, all employees need to be supported in their personal lives. If your flexibility policies exclude a segment of your workforce, you're doing something wrong.

Prioritize clear structures and policies

If you were to randomly ask leaders or employees at your company to describe flexibility, they should be able to give a clear answer—and their answers should be consistent. Flexibility policies will not work if they are difficult to understand, if employees or managers don't know how to use them, or if they vary greatly in approach. Organizations benefit when they develop clear, written frameworks with principles that can guide decision making about and expectations for flexibility. These frameworks should be communicated widely.

As an example, here's a brief checklist that draws from the employee assistance program at LifeWorks (formerly Morneau Shepell) and can serve as a starting point for any company's flexible work arrangements:

- Develop a written policy that clearly lays out expectations.

- Communicate with all employees about the possibilities for flexible work, and aim to achieve equality.

- Ask employees to document their planned versus actual work hours to foster work routines and increase transparency about when they are working and when they are off.

- Use clear metrics to evaluate employees on the *quality* of their work, not the timing or quantity of it.

Manager checklists like this one are becoming widespread. In Canada, as in the United Kingdom and Australia, the right to request a flexible schedule is gaining legal ground.

Within these guidelines, the manager's role is to match flexible work processes with customer, product creation, and service demands. Thus leaders must understand how each type of flexibility—schedule, place, continuity, workload, and mode—aligns with the job at hand, their employees, and policies. As figure 1-1, "A flexibility primer," shows, various combinations of flexible arrangements may have bundling synergies. For example, location and schedule flexibility sometimes work well in combination.

The choices made must be viewed as fair by both leaders and employees. Studies show that when they are, workers who experience work-family conflict remain committed to their organizations.[1]

FIGURE 1-1

A flexibility primer

Five different types of flexibility your organization can consider and how they might be bundled.

Policy type	Policy examples	Bundling option	Employee benefits	Employer benefits
Schedule Employees can vary their schedules to meet daily, weekly, or monthly expectations.	• Flex time • Compressed workweek • Shift swapping • Shift scheduling	Schedule Place Continuity Workload	• More control over days or hours worked • Less time commuting • Greater ability to meet non-work needs during regular work hours • Greater feeling of control	• Greater producti-vity and employee focus • Less absente-eism • Less overtime
Place Employees can work away from their employer's work site using technology or other types of communication tools.	• Telework (using tech-nology to work from any location) • Remote work (living out-side the geographic area of the employer) • Telecommut-ing (working from home) • Hoteling/ satellite offices	Schedule Place	• Less time commuting locally • Less exhaustion from global or national trips • Freedom to live closer to family or friends	• Less turnover • Lower overhead costs • Larger talent pool

Policy type	Policy examples	Bundling option	Employee benefits	Employer benefits
Continutity Employees can choose when to take time off without losing their jobs.	• Leaves (family, sick, maternity, paternity, education, military)	Schedule Continuity Workload	• Time to give birth, care for a child or parent, attend school, serve in the military, or recover from illness • Ability to return to work sooner when combined with job sharing or part-time work • Less burnout • Time to nurse or bond with a child	• Less turnover • Greater retention of quality employees
Workload Employees can opt for a less-than-full-time schedule in return for a commensurate cut in pay.	• Job share • Part-time work • Lighter workload	Schedule Workload	• Less overload or burnout • Decreased work-family conflict	• Less turnover • Greater retention of quality employees
Mode Employees can vary the degree to which they work off-site.	• Site work • Hybrid • Remote	Schedule Place Continuity Workload Mode	• Ability to coordinate and accomplish work using technology • Ability to mix modes for varying types of work tasks	• Greater productivity • Lower office space costs

Source: "Flexible work schedules," by E. E. Kossek and J. S. Michel (2009); "A Review of Telework Research," by D. E. Bailey and N. B. Kurland; and "Balanced Flexibility," by E. E. Kossek, R. Thompson, and B. Lautsch (2015).

How can managers cultivate this kind of environment and roll out flexible policies fairly? One way is to develop a team charter, as the financial services firm Northern Trust a number of years ago[2] did for units migrating to a flexible work mode. Questions that leaders, team members, and other stakeholders might discuss include the following:

- How has the company decided to manage location-based pay equity? For example, will all fully remote workers who perform the same jobs, regardless of whether they live in Tulsa or Los Angeles, receive the same base and merit pay?

- What are fair criteria for how the team sets core hours—say, from 10 a.m. to 3 p.m.—around when members will be available for collaboration, meetings, and communication?

- What is an equitable way to set limits on employees' availability, and what are norms for respecting time off?

Although clear policies and consistent implementation are important, overly restrictive policies are not the answer. Processes should be adaptable.

Empower employees to create and manage their own flexibility

Although leaders must help shape the structures and policies for flexible work, they don't need to have all the answers. Instead, they should facilitate conversations with workers to unpack all the ways in which people interpret flexibility—from where one works to the construction of one's work schedule. It may be helpful for managers to give employees a list of considerations to reflect on and address. Here are some examples:

- How might my clients' experience be affected by my flexibility? In what ways can any negative impact be mitigated?

- How might my interactions with team members be affected? What actions can I take to ensure strong collaboration and working relationships?

- Do I have, or can I develop, the skills I need for the proposed flexible work arrangement? For example, do I have the self-discipline to manage attention and boundaries for telework or to maintain the energy and focus for a compressed workweek?

- Have I talked with my manager and clients to ensure that my part-time job is designed and scoped realistically so that I can perform it effectively within my reduced hours?

- Do I have the right work and home resources (tech support, an internet connection, space, family support, a backup work location) to ensure that I can accomplish my job?

The next step is to create organization-wide structures for self-scheduling and shift swapping to empower employees. Rather than making supervisors pivotal in managing the everyday implementation of flexibility, some industries are setting up employee self-management processes that give workers greater control over their schedules and hours without penalty.

Health care organizations in particular, with their largely female workforces, have been early adopters of self-scheduling. In one study of self-scheduling among nurses in five comparable medical and surgical units, a key component of its success was educating them about self-scheduling and negotiation skills and when to adjust guidelines to meet needs, such as determining holiday coverage.[3] Employee satisfaction and retention increased as a result.

Another example comes from Delta, a large, non-unionized U.S. airline that employs a "bidding" process whereby employees pick their own shifts using a software program, with choice increasing according to seniority. Workers may swap or give away shifts as long as overtime doesn't increase and health and safety rules are not violated.

In both of these examples, the role of leaders is to establish guidelines regarding what works and what doesn't in a way that is facilitating but not controlling, ensuring that workers understand their accountability for guaranteeing staffing mandates and, in the case of health care, the quality of patient care. Companies moving to widespread flexible remote-work systems can learn a lot from health care organizations and Delta.

Remove disincentives for use

Policies that enable employees to freely take vacation when desired or sick leave when needed are often accompanied by disincentives for using them. (Consider the "unlimited vacation time" that no one actually takes advantage of.) A common barrier is chronic understaffing. In a study we conducted of frontline workers, only one in four employees at a continuously running oil production company could use available vacation time because of it. As a result, employees suffered burnout. One manager reported being unable to get time off to attend a niece's wedding, even though he was supposed to walk her down the aisle in place of her late father. We also see structural disincentives in health care, where nurses are increasingly unable to use paid vacation and sick time earned, and we have encountered leave incentive programs in which employees can actually make *more* money by not taking time off.

Many organizational cultures disincentivize the use of time-off policies for nonwork needs as well. In one case, a department chair celebrated a male professor for attending a faculty meeting during parental leave, whereas a female colleague who had just given birth missed the meeting to nurse the baby and recover. The message to employees was clear: You are rewarded for showing up even when the official policy says you're not supposed to.

Leaders must remove both types of disincentives. One tactic is to publicly recognize top employees who work flexibly and achieve high performance. In one of our studies, a lawyer who was working reduced hours won an Employee of the Year award by discovering a way to save the firm a great deal of money.

We've also seen some companies use flexibility as an incentive to reduce excessive overtime and burnout and increase productivity and cost savings. One pharmaceutical company offered employees workweeks of four 10-hour days with job security in return for a no-overtime-payment agreement. The company saved money *and* saw improved performance as the team became self-managing and supervisors transitioned out of boss roles and became team members themselves. The former supervisors responded positively because they no longer had to manage the overtime needs of the organization, could work just four days a week, and felt more integrated and supported on their teams.

Remember that leadership matters

True flexibility that meets business and personal needs is unlikely to succeed without support from the top. An example comes from GM CEO Mary Barra's post-pandemic call to "work appropriately." "Where the work permits," she said, "employees have the flexibility to work where they can have the greatest impact on achieving our goals . . . It is up to leaders to focus on the work, not the where, and we will provide the tools and resources needed to make the right decisions to support our teams."[4]

The jury is still out on how successful GM and other firms—such as Google—that take similar approaches will be, but it's encouraging to hear CEOs strategically setting the tone for flexibility by making it the rule rather than the exception. Top leaders can also recognize and reward supervisors who encourage their teams to get the work done without burning out.

Leaders must be careful in how they talk about various forms of flexibility. For example, when teleworking is framed as an initiative to improve work-family balance, it often becomes a gendered phenomenon, leading men to assume they can't take advantage of it or to conceal that they're doing it for work-life reasons, to avoid being stigmatized. So it's important to communicate examples of increased flexibility's effectiveness for all kinds of workers in all kinds of jobs and at all levels.

Leaders must also explain the organization's commitment to flexibility to outside stakeholders. For example, if a company is practicing flexibility but its clients still expect 24/7 responses, the company's policy simply won't work. One way to address this issue is to bake client expectations into flexible work plans—for example, by staffing key accounts with several employees who can tag-team and then presenting that as a benefit to clients.

Experiment and measure outcomes, including equity

True flexibility is an ongoing process requiring that management be open to experimentation and new ideas. Some arrangements may not work at first and will need to be adjusted. That is normal and an important part of the process; evolution does not equate with failure. For example, Microsoft found that when a large team initially moved to remote work in 2020, employees worked an average of four more hours a week, sent more messages at nonstandard hours, and spent more time in meetings (albeit shorter ones), risking burnout. Leaders soon realized that this pace was unsustainable—for themselves and for employees—and encouraged teams to develop guidelines to ensure boundaries between work and nonwork time (clear-cut shifts, daily breaks, and dedicated solo work hours, for example).

At the same time, evidence suggests that gathering data and making changes can pay off. Northern Trust migrated entire job functions and teams to hybrid remote work (with at least one day in the office and at least one day at home) years before the pandemic. It used pre- and post-evaluation tools to assess whether jobs could be done securely and teams could work effectively regardless of location. Migrating, piloting, and evaluating departments one at a time, the company shifted its culture toward more-flexible working by systematically accumulating data to support its approach while fine-tuning for each work unit. It saved millions of dollars by reducing office space around the world, and employee stress plummeted as a result of less commuting.

Consider the impact of flexibility on your global workforce

In interviews with an oil company in the EU, we found that employees in one of the company's Asian offices preferred a 3 p.m. to 12 a.m. workday. That allowed many workers to pick up their children from school, facilitated communication across time zones, and increased employee productivity and engagement. For example, no one had to get up in the middle of the night for a conference call, since 3 p.m. in the Asia office was 9 a.m. at the company's headquarters. Such localized flexibility practices can help maintain equity among employees in different parts of the world so that team members work at mutually convenient times.

To ensure fair access and results as your company experiments, conduct doing an audit to see whether heavier users of work-life flexibility have pay equity, and be sure to take race and gender into consideration. There's evidence that inequity can and does occur. For instance, in 2019 the bonuses of senior female employees who took maternity leave at the Swiss bank UBS were not restored to previous levels when they returned. Some of them eventually resigned. Another example comes from Nike, which cut pay for star athletes who went on maternity leave. (After a backlash, the company adjusted that policy to avoid penalizing mothers.)

We caution against establishing a policy that offers employees the option of remote work only if they take a pay cut or creating a pay structure that's based on location. Talent is talent, and compensation shouldn't depend on where employees are unless their location is vital for the people they're serving (say, in government) or required by licensing rules (say, in law). Such policies are also likely to drive more women to unemployment, and result in a 'shecession' as Nicole Mason, the president and CEO of the Institute of Women's Policy Research aptly calls it.[5] Calibrating pay according to choice of work location can make the shecession even worse and increase the gender pay gap, because women are 50% more likely than men to apply for remote work. They also use flexibility more often, take on more school and childcare logistical management during the workday, and are more likely to be the trailing spouse when couples coordinate dual careers, thus trading geographical location for remote work.

Finally, remember that implementing flexibility involves a learning curve

The leader's role is to make performance expectations clear, offer resources to support flexibility, and ensure performance is consistent across people and teams. If someone is falling short, put that person on a performance-improvement plan and assess whether skills, motivation, or some other issue is getting in the way. Don't assume that flexibility is the main reason that work isn't getting done.

Leaders need to stop viewing flexibility as an HR policy and regard it as an opportunity for organizational transformation that will benefit both their employees and their businesses.

Ellen Ernst Kossek is the Basil S. Turner Distinguished Professor of Management at Purdue University, and formerly was president of the Work and Family Researchers Network. She studies how leaders' support of work-life boundaries, flexibility, and remote work affects women's inclusion and career equality.

Patricia Gettings is an assistant professor of communication at the State University of New York at Albany. She studies the intersections of personal relationships and organizational commitments and how individuals and organizations negotiate those overlaps.

Kaumudi Misra is an associate professor of management at California State University, East Bay. She studies the role of work-life flexibility practices as a strategic human resource lever for individual and organizational productivity.

NOTES

1. Phyllis A. Siegel et al., "The Moderating Influence of Procedural Fairness on the Relationship Between Work-Life Conflict and Organizational Commitment," *Journal of Applied Psychology* 90, no. 1 (2005): 13–24.

2. Ellen Ernst Kossek, Rebecca J. Thompson, and Brenda A. Lautsch, "Balanced Workplace Flexibility: Avoiding the Traps," *California Management Review* 57, no. 4 (August 1, 2015), https://journals .sagepub.com/doi/abs/10.1525/cmr.2015.57.4.5.

3. Nancy Hoffart and Sara Willdermood, "Self-Scheduling in Five Med/Surg Units: A Comparison," *Nurse Management* 28, no. 4 (1997): 42–27.

4. Mary Barra, "Embracing a New Way of Working," LinkedIn, April 20, 2021, https://www.linkedin.com/pulse/embracing-new-way -working-mary-barra.

5. Alisha Haridasani Gupta, "Why Some Women Call This Recession a 'Shecession,'" *New York Times*, June 18, 2021, https://www .nytimes.com/2020/05/09/us/unemployment-coronavirus-women .html.

CHAPTER 2

What Mix of WFH and Office Time Is Right for You?

by Robert C. Pozen and Alexandra Samuel

Many of us have things to love about working from home, like flexibility, the ability to focus, and no commute. But there is a lot to love about the office, too: social interaction, the joys of collaboration, and, of course, that endless pot of coffee.

Many companies intend to give us the best of both worlds by allowing employees to split their time between home and the workplace. But it will only give *you* the best of both worlds if you figure out how to combine

Adapted from content posted on hbr.org, May 4, 2021 (product #H06C44).

home and office time in a way that maximizes your productivity and personal well-being. That means figuring out which days to spend at home, which to spend at the office, and, just as crucial, how to sell your boss on that plan.

The key is identifying which parts of your job are best accomplished where. This seems simple enough: For tasks that require collaboration, go into work; for tasks that require extended concentration, stay home. And, true enough, a review of research on virtual teams reported that multiple studies show highly interdependent work can be difficult to tackle when you're separated from your colleagues.[1] But one of the studies also found that close collaboration across distance actually strengthened relationships and engagement among colleagues, because it required them to improve their communication and mutual support.

There are other factors at play, too. For example, maybe you do your best drafting work at home—but you need the collaboration of your colleagues to develop an initial outline. Or maybe you actually find it easier to brainstorm over a phone call, since you're most creative while pacing the room.

No matter which factors most affect you, you'll want to avoid wasting critical time by coming into the office on a day it would have been better to stay at home, or vice versa. To create a hybrid work plan that allows you to get the most out of each day, first track and analyze your work to figure out which factors affect your productivity. Then match up your findings with your tasks and responsibilities. Finally, summarize your plan for your boss to get their buy-in.

Track Metrics That Matter

To track your productivity in each location, you need to determine what to measure. We tend to think of productivity in terms of hours worked, but a more effective measure is the actual results of your labors. For hard metrics, look for some output measurements (words typed, emails answered, tasks checked off) as well as data on how your time gets used (we like automatic time-tracker apps like Timing or ManicTime). For soft metrics, consider logging both your mood and your sense of accomplishment at the end of each day (use a 1-to-5 scale); you can also use things like email or group messaging to track feedback from others. None of these indicators is perfect, but together they present a useful picture.

Set up a spreadsheet where you can consolidate all your metrics into a single view. The simplest approach is to list the dates in the first column on the left and then assign a column to each key metric, like words typed, mood, accomplishments, and tasks completed. You might also want to track how much time you're wasting on distractions (online shopping, meme browsing, gaming), how much you're spending on meetings, and how much you're spending in apps that indicate you are working diligently (like your word processor or spreadsheet app).

Then, for a limited period—roughly a month or two—track your daily productivity along each of the metrics you've defined. You can start this process even before you return to the office: Track your productivity metrics while working remotely, and then when you get back to your office you'll have a baseline that will make it easy to quickly compare your productivity in each space. During your tracking period, mark the spreadsheet every single day to note whether you're working remotely or in the office (or commit to a specific schedule); otherwise you'll have no way of spotting the patterns that separate office days from home days.

Look for Patterns

Once it's time to crunch the numbers, just eyeballing the columns of your spreadsheet will give you a sense of where you need to dig into the data more deeply. If your productive time or mood varies wildly from day to day, for example, you might scan for something that seems to correlate with those variations—perhaps the amount of time you spend in meetings, or your sleep hours.

To perform a deeper analysis, create a table or chart that zooms in on the relationship between the variations in your mood or output and the factor(s) you think may explain those variations. Maybe you get more tasks completed on days with fewer meetings . . . unless the meetings take place in the two hours after lunch, when you struggle to get focused work done anyhow. Maybe the days with the most "wasted" time are also the days when you generate the most written work, because all those little distractions are the way you reboot in between pages, documents, or paragraphs.

Look especially for any divergences between your home days and your office days. Are there certain kinds of tasks that you complete more quickly at home, or at the office? Do meetings have the same impact on your mood or productivity when they're face to face, rather than held via video? Do your most productive work times differ depending on when you're working?

The answer may depend on the flow of life at home just as much as on the distractions of the office.

Once you know which kinds of tasks you do best at home and at the office, you'll be in a better position to judge how to spend each day. And you can get a sense of the big picture, too: Review your current responsibilities and determine how much of your workload is best handled in each location to decide how much time you'll want to spend there. This is a process you may need to revisit periodically: Perhaps this quarter's big project involves planning a conference, which is a very collaborative process that will benefit from more time in the office. But maybe next quarter you are producing the company's annual report, which will require more time at home so that you can do focused writing and revising.

Making the Case for Your Hybrid Plan

Knowing where you want to spend your time is all well and good, but it won't help if your boss isn't on board with your hybrid work plan. Luckily, all the data you've crunched about your productivity gives you a great place to start making the case. Summarize your findings in a concise note that shows the major responsibilities on your plate and breaks them out into the parts that are best handled at the office and the parts that are best handled at home. Support your conclusions with data that shows you write more words, reply to more emails, or create presentations more efficiently on the days that you are at home.

Depending on your manager, you may also find it helpful to estimate the specific amount of time each part of your work is likely to require.

For example, if your upcoming responsibilities include leading the work on that annual report, your hybrid plan might look like table 2-1. Based on this breakdown, about one-third of your time on this project should be spent in the office, and two-thirds can be better spent at home. If your other responsibilities have a similar breakdown, you might propose spending three days a week working remotely and two days a week at the office—with those days scheduled to facilitate your stakeholder interviews and project meetings.

If your boss is still skeptical of the value of remote work, suggest a trial period of a month or so to follow

TABLE 2-1

Annual report (68 hours)

Office tasks (24 hours)	Remote tasks (44 hours)
• Interview stakeholders (12 hours)	• Background research for content (14 hours)
• Brainstorm report messages (1 hour)	• Draft report content (16 hours)
• Outline report (2 hours)	• Image research for report design (4 hours)
• Review/troubleshoot report drafts (6 hours)	• Review/edit final report (10 hours)
• Brief and update designer (3 hours)	

your proposed combination of days at home and at the office. By the end of the month, your excellent results should win over your boss. That's what happened to Maggie Crowley Sheehan, who was the first employee at software company Unbounce to go remote, long before the pandemic. When her husband got a job in the Bahamas, Sheehan's supervisor agreed to make her a test case for remote work. Her results were so strong that when the rest of the company went remote during Covid-19, one of Sheehan's colleagues said, "We're all going to become 80% more productive now—just look at what happened with Maggie!"

By thinking through the mix of home and office work that will allow you to be the most productive, you'll avoid frustration in both locations—and demonstrate to your boss your ability to take ownership of your working conditions and productivity in the new hybrid workplace.

Robert C. Pozen is a senior lecturer at MIT's Sloan School of Management, a former president of Fidelity Investments, and a nonresident senior fellow at the Brookings Institution. He is an author, with Alexandra Samuel, of *Remote, Inc.: How to Thrive at Work . . . Wherever You Are.*

Alexandra Samuel is a tech speaker and data journalist who creates data-driven reports and workshops for companies around the world. She is an author, with Robert C. Pozen, of *Remote, Inc.: How to Thrive at Work*

. . . *Wherever You Are* and the author of *Work Smarter with Social Media.* Follow her on Twitter: @awsamuel.

NOTE

1. Sarah Morrison-Smith and Jaime Ruiz, "Challenges and Barriers in Virtual Teams: A Literature Review," *SN Applied Sciences* 2 (2020): 1096. https://link.springer.com/article/10.1007%2Fs42452 -020-2801-5.

CHAPTER 3

Set a Hybrid Schedule That Works for You

by Elizabeth Grace Saunders

If you find yourself in the situation where you're able or required to have some in-person face time each week and you feel uncertain about what you should request, here are some strategies that can help guide your hybrid schedule decisions. As a time-management coach, I find that considering these four key factors can empower you to maximize your overall productivity when you're (partially) figuring out how to balance your working locations.

Adapted from "How to Set a Hybrid Work Schedule That Works for You," on hbr.org, October 14, 2021 (product #H06LNV).

What Tasks Do I Prefer to Do in the Office?

Some of the most important business functions happen most effectively in person. Whenever possible, you'll want to be literally "at the table" when it comes to high-level strategic decisions and negotiations. What's communicated—and not communicated—virtually is substantively different from what happens in person.

But even if you're not making game-changing decisions, there are tasks you may prefer to do in the office. For example, if you have project meetings that require problem solving, decision making, or reviewing tangible objects, or that have highly emotional content, those are best done in person. Schedule your in-office days for when those project meetings are held. And if you have some authority over those meetings, consider asking other team members to try to make it into the office on those days as well. You could also tweak these preferences over time. For example, have everyone meet in person when you're first kicking off the project, hold virtual meetings for standard updates, and then encourage people to come in person again when it's time for a more in-depth review of deliverables.

When Does My Team Need Me?

To maximize your team productivity, you'll also want to identify what kind of interactions (in-person or virtual) will be most effective. If some of your colleagues—and specifically, your direct reports—better comprehend what you are saying and retain and respond to the information more appropriately when you're in person, try to plan some in-office days to align with when those individuals will also be present. Thirty minutes spent in person could save you hours of headache from unread or misunderstood written and phone communication. Alternatively, if you discover that some of your colleagues comprehend information better in writing or through some other virtual method, continue having those meetings remotely and reserve your in-office time for other activities.

Despite all of us having honed our virtual communication skills during the pandemic, people may have preferences for in-person communication, face-to-face meetings, or remote options, so consider what makes sense for each individual on your team as you look at your schedule.

How Can I Maximize My Productivity?

The first two factors I shared have to do with maximizing your productivity on project work. But the final two factors are about maximizing your personal productivity, starting with managing your energy.

If you have more introverted tendencies, you may find it effective to do no more than two days in a row in the office. For example, maybe you decide to go in Monday, Tuesday, Thursday or Monday, Wednesday, Friday. By interspersing your days in the office with days at home, you give yourself an opportunity to recharge by having less stimulation from other people on your remote days. You can also group together your meetings on the days you're in the office so that your work-from-home days have longer stretches of uninterrupted time for getting your solo work done.

On the other hand, if you have more extroverted tendencies, going into the office multiple days in a row may not be a problem. And you may be energized by booking meetings both when you're in the office and at home so that you have opportunities to connect with people daily. When you are working remotely, book some meetings at the start of your workday to get you geared up and then again in the afternoon when your energy starts to wane.

When Do I Feel the Least Motivated?

Even prior to the exodus from the office, I saw that my coaching clients tend to have motivation trends throughout the week. For some, they start out Monday morning with a bang, but by Friday afternoon it's extraordinarily difficult for them to get any substantive work done. For others, it's the opposite: It takes them a while to get going on Monday, but by Friday they're knocking things off the list easily and working until 6 or 7 p.m. at night.

Remote work can affect these motivation levels as well, especially if you're younger. A Pew Research Center study that measured the grand shift to remote work found that 42% of workers ages 18 to 49 said that it had been difficult to feel motivated to do their work remotely. And the percentage is even higher for those ages 18 to 29, with 53% saying it was difficult to do their work when they weren't in person with their colleagues. (This is in contrast to only 20% of workers 50 and older feeling the same way.)

Use in-office days to balance out those times when you're feeling less motivated. Just like going to the gym can make it massively easier to exercise, going to the office makes it massively easier to get work done for some people. If you find you're most motivated when you're around other people and you fade as the week progresses, request regular office days on Thursday and Friday. If you find the opposite to be true, and know that you'll get a lot more done if you go in Monday and Tuesday, make that your aim. Know when you'll need some positive peer pressure, and plan your hybrid schedule accordingly for big increases in productivity.

With more and more organizations making the shift to remote and hybrid arrangements, you're likely facing the possibility of a schedule that bridges in-person and remote work. Consider these four factors when making your decision on when to be in the office so that being in the workplace works for you.

Elizabeth Grace Saunders is a time management coach and the founder of Real Life E Time Coaching & Speaking. She is the author of *How to Invest Your Time Like Money* and *Divine Time Management*. Find out more at www.RealLifeE.com.

SECTION TWO

Making the Ask

CHAPTER 4

How to Negotiate a Remote Arrangement with Your Boss

by Ruchi Sinha and Carol T. Kulik

More businesses and companies have adopted flexible work arrangements on a grand scale. Employees who never thought of working from home before are experiencing a newfound love for the flexibility that remote work can offer.

Have you been considering making the ask and negotiating a remote and flexible work arrangement with your boss? If so, how should you go about it?

Adapted from "How to Negotiate Remote and Flexible Work Arrangements with Your Boss," on hbr.org, June 9, 2020.

First, let's look at two myths about negotiating flexible work arrangements.

Myth 1: Negotiating flexibility is mainly about when and where you do your work

There is a tendency to view flexibility negotiations as revolving around only the hours you work and the location from which you work. But flexibility is also determined by the nature of the tasks that make up your job role. Some tasks are better performed remotely than others. When you negotiate flexibility, you need to negotiate what work you will do, how your work fits into the bigger picture, and how it will be evaluated.

One way to do so is job crafting, a process of arranging your work responsibilities to better fit your needs, strengths, and passions. When you discuss your tasks or role with your boss, think about the scope of your responsibilities, the logistics of how you will interact and coordinate with other members of your team, and how you and your team's role performance and objectives will be monitored and evaluated.

It is within these conversations that you can bring up the feasibility and effectiveness of flexible work—laying the foundation to negotiate where and when you do your job. For example, you might make a case to bundle certain tasks and deliverables in a way that allows you to complete them away from the office, or you might take up some new responsibilities and give away others to shape your role to suit your flexible schedule.

Myth 2: Negotiating flexibility is only possible when your organization has an explicit policy supporting flexible work

Research shows that employees can adopt three different strategies for negotiating work flexibility—asking, bending, and shaping.[1]

Asking is easy when your company already has a clear organizational policy for you to work remotely. You simply ask your manager.

Bending is a negotiation strategy where you ask for flexibility as an exception to the rule. Your organization may not have a flexibility policy, or you may want a specific type of flexibility for which there is no policy and no precedent. For example, maybe you are living with an elderly parent who needs regular daytime care, and due to this you ask to work from 7 a.m. to 10 a.m. and then from 5 p.m. to 10 p.m.

Shaping is a type of negotiation where you attempt to change the organizational policy by making a flexibility case not just for yourself but for a larger collective. Maybe you have realized that your team collaboration is much more efficient remotely, and as a team you want to leverage a remote arrangement.

All three are possible, and your workplace may be the perfect testing ground for bending and shaping requests. If you are well prepared and understand how flexibility will impact your role productivity and that of your team, you are likely to succeed in these negotiations.

How to ask your boss for a flexible work arrangement

1. Understand your organization's policies (if they exist).

Review your firm's current policies around flexible work arrangements, and understand when and why your firm developed them. Consider the compliance and work-health safety risks of remote work that apply to your firm. Identify the teams and employees who have made the most use of flexible work, along with the common features they share. Speak with trusted mentors and team members to understand how flexibility may be linked to other employment issues such as compensation and benefits, performance evaluation, promotion, training, employer regulation, etc. This understanding will help you know whether your ask will be seen as a bending or a shaping request. It will also help you to prepare offers that can mitigate potential risks—making it easier for your employer to say "yes."

2. Understand your role and its relationship to the roles of your team members.

Think about how your job fits with those of other members of your team. Talk to your coworkers about your shared responsibilities, how they get work done, and their preferred work schedules.

Divide the tasks into face-to-face and remote. Prepare a table summarizing the essential tasks that require face-to-face interactions and tasks that can be managed remotely. For all tasks that can be managed remotely, speak with your team members to identify technology and tools that will enable better remote collaboration. This will provide you with information on how your flexibility might influence both your and your team's role execution.

3. Document your successes with flexibility.

Create a file of evidence on how you have coordinated with your team and accomplished your goals while working remotely. Document your fluency in virtual collaboration.

For example, was there a project on the back burner that you fast-tracked while working from home because you were able to immerse yourself in it and engage in strategic thinking? Examples like these build an evidence-based case and give you an opportunity to ask for specific equipment (tools and technology) to be more productive in your home office.

4. Have a plan B in place.

Think about the potential constraints and sticking points that your boss might bring up. Keep in mind your boss's interests and concerns, and the potential benefits of giving you flexibility. Consider presenting the flexibility ask as an experiment wherein you offer to engage in remote work for three or six months with regular reporting on your progress and an agreed-upon definition of the performance criteria. By offering your boss more data and greater accountability, you are likely to lower the sense of risk.

Remember, your success at the negotiation table is determined by the mindset you have on what is and is not possible and by how you do the groundwork and preparation before the conversation, rather than just how tough you are at the table. These steps will aid you in presenting a more durable case for your flexibility ask.

———————

Ruchi Sinha is an associate professor of management at the University of South Australia Business School. Her research explores how voice, trust, conflict, and power dynamics influence work and negotiation outcomes.

Carol T. Kulik is a research professor of human resource management at University of South Australia Business School. Her research investigates how disadvantaged employees can negotiate employment arrangements that benefit both parties in the employment relationship.

NOTE

1. Hannah Riley Bowles, Bobbi J. Thomason, and Julia B. Bear, "Reconceptualizing What and How Women Negotiate for Career Advancement," *Academy of Management Journal* 62 (2019): 1645–1671.

CHAPTER 5

Adventures in Alternative Work Arrangements

by Michele Benton

Before having kids, we tend to envision ourselves as the devoted company worker, always present, fully committed, and willing to give extra effort to get the job done. But with children come new demands, especially for the majority of us who are in dual-career households. Our commitment and career ambitions hold true; it's just harder to fit life around traditional work structures. It would seem that alternative work programs—flexible hours, remote work, part-time salaried work, job shares,

Adapted from content posted on hbr.org, July 7, 2020 (product #H05PCB).

and lateral moves—create a win-win for employers, employees, and families.

Unfortunately, alternative work is a bit of a ruse. Most employers offer it, usually as part of their inclusion programs to attract quality talent (you!). But often it's an empty gesture, as few employees ever use the option. Research in the U.S. and Europe confirms consequences we already know: Using these programs means certain career death.

Yet we desperately need these options—not on paper, but in practice in our lives. With no yellow brick road to follow, we must find our own way forward. Here are four steps to making an alternative work program work for you.

Get real

Just because a company is recognized as a top employer for parents doesn't mean alternative work is mainstream. Often it functions like a glorified mommy track, and access is based on manager preference (plus, what works in one department may not work in yours). In developing your alternative work proposal, look around, chat with colleagues, and tap into HR to assess potential acceptance and barriers:

- Do senior leaders "get it"? How many are parents of young children or part of a dual-career couple? What unstated messages are sent about family and work?

- What types of alternative work are accepted? Is it only "work from home Fridays" or are other types commonplace? Which departments or roles permit it? Are certain managers more accepting?

- What happens to people who use alternative work? How do they get big projects or promotions? Do they have a senior-level sponsor, a plan to ramp back up, or something else for support?

Make it worthwhile

Build on areas of acceptance and overcome barriers by helping your leaders realize there are different ways to show career commitment:

- **Craft a value proposition.** Assess what impact you have on revenue, profit, efficiency, or costs, and connect it to your proposal. For example, maybe your part-time role saves $1 million in outside vendor fees, working three days remote delivers $300,000 in sales, or a lateral move closes a gap without the costs/downtime of hiring a temp. Be creative—for ideas, tap a finance friend.

- **Talk outcomes, not hours.** Many cultures tend to focus on busyness, time, or effort when discussing work. Instead, highlight your efficient methods, innovative use of resources, or creative thinking skills. (Think of yourself as a consultant who charges by project deliverable, not billable hours.) During performance reviews, champion your accomplishments and make the case for a meaningful salary increase and bonus. Steer conversations toward your bottom-line value.

- **Protect what you hope to gain.** If your goal is fewer hours, don't automatically work longer than agreed or overcompensate in a frenzy while at work. If you want less intensity in your lateral position, make sure an additional project brings promotable skills or senior stakeholder visibility before you take it on. Be selective when giving discretionary effort.

- **Make it normal.** Avoid signaling that alternative work is wrong. You wouldn't apologize to colleagues if you weren't available one evening or on a Sunday morning, so don't apologize for not working conventional hours. Simply state what's possible: "I'm not available Monday, but I'm open 9–2 on Tuesday." Or, "I can have it ready Friday, would that work?"

- **Push for career support.** Seek senior-level mentors and talk up how your alternative work arrangement is creating results. Before talent discussions, check in with your manager to prepare them to advocate for you. Let decision makers know you're interested in high-potential leadership training and resources.

Buck gender assumptions

Even though family structures have evolved into countless variations, stereotypes of life divided between a working husband and a stay-at-home wife linger. With alternative work programs, men get the benefit of the doubt, whereas women get punished because motherhood seems incompatible with work commitment. At home, alternative work for women usually translates into more domestic burdens, like childcare or housework, but for most men, it facilitates other work arenas like training or a side gig. Consider how gender assumptions intersect with the life you're trying to create:

- When changing job structures, be clear about what things you're taking on outside of work. Make sure you and your partner feel expectations and trade-offs are fair, and frame shared duties the same way (is it parenting or babysitting?).

- A lot of advice today encourages women to recast their definition of success away from power and money, to things like well-being or family satisfaction, and to be at peace with dropping the ball or opting out. Define success for yourself.

Vote with your feet

Finally, if you can't get support for an alternative program that works for you, take your talent elsewhere. Reallocate discretionary time to job searching. In your exit interview, tell HR exactly why you're leaving, as company execs read these reports.

When it comes to creating career opportunities that support your life and goals outside of work, your words and actions can help transform alternative work from good policy to good practice.

––––––––

Michele Benton is founder and CEO of lime LLC, a global life sciences marketing strategy, training, and capabilities company delivering proven marketing ingredients to grow profits. Her team is crafting their own future-forward workplace that creates meaningful, groundbreaking client value without the constraints of the traditional corporate grind. Come follow Michele's adventures in the new normal of alternative work at: www.linkedin.com/in/michelebenton/.

CHAPTER 6

Asking Your Boss for a Four-Day Workweek

by Joe Sanok

Imagine living in a world of forever three-day weekends.

In college, I got a glimpse of that reality.

Freshman year, my academic adviser informed me and my peers that we could plan our own schedules, and I used my newfound agency to enroll in classes Monday through Thursday, leaving Fridays completely free. Over the next three years, I maintained that schedule—until I graduated and got my first job.

Adapted from "How to Ask Your Boss For a 4-Day Workweek," on hbr .org, September 3, 2021.

Like most employers in America, the nonprofit that hired me encouraged its workers to put in eight hours a day, five days a week. Over time, leadership recognized what I discovered during undergrad: People are more productive when we have the option to work flexibly. I was able to negotiate a four-day workweek, but the experience was largely an exception.

As I grew in my career, I shifted back to a long week and put in more hours, often to the point of burning out. It wasn't until a few years ago that I decided to quit full-time work, set up my own consultancy practice, and reclaim control over my schedule.

While I found my way back, I wasted years miserably grinding to climb the proverbial career ladder. If you find yourself in a similar position, here's what I want you to know: You don't have to work a certain number of hours to be productive. The concept of "time" is entirely human-made, the classification of a "week" is arbitrary, and if you look back far enough, you'll see that the 40-hour workweek is a short-lived phenomenon.

Let me explain . . .

The Random History of Time and Labor

Several thousand years ago, every civilization had its own measure of time. The Romans, for instance, had a 10-day week. The neighboring Egyptians followed a calendar with eight days in a week. The seven-day week as we know it was created by the Babylonians, who believed in seven celestial bodies (the sun, the moon, Mercury, Venus, Mars, Jupiter, Saturn). This concept slowly spread around the world to other cultures, including the Jews, the Persian Empire, the Greeks, and finally the Romans, who made it official.

The five-day workweek only became a thing in the early twentieth century.

Well into the Industrial Revolution, the average employee worked 10 to 14 hours a day for six to seven days a week. This went on through the early 1900s, when employees finally began to form unions, and despite being met with much resistance from their employers, they demanded shorter workdays. The demand was partly a result of scarce opportunities that had to be shared among a large workforce. Shorter workdays were expected to create more demand for workers and also boost their wages.

A major shift, however, occurred in 1926, when Henry Ford's car company, Ford Motor Co., switched to a 40-hour workweek. But Ford's decision was not driven by generosity or care for his employee's well-being. He wanted to sell cars to his own workers, who he believed would be better customers if they had more time off (and he was right).

The 40-hour workweek has stayed with us since.

My point is this: While the 9-to-5 job feels preordained, it's based on an exploitative model less than 100 years old, and it's about time we rethink it.

The Case for a Four-Day Workweek

Remember a few minutes ago when you imagined that glorious life with a permanent three-day weekend? Well, in some countries, people are already living out your dream.

Iceland conducted a trial of 2,500 workers who switched from 40 hours per week to 35 or 36 hours. The results confirmed that shorter workweeks improved work-life balance. Further, participants reported feeling less burned out and more productive and happier. Now, countries like Spain, Denmark, and New Zealand are following suit.

The four-day workweek is not a new concept, but Covid and its impact on the corporate world have been a catalyst for its gaining popularity. The work-from-home arrangement during the pandemic pushed many of us to question the industrialist model of going into the office every day. It has also made us rethink what we want our workplace to look like. Employees are asking for more flexibility in the way they organize their time— and for good reason.

Numerous studies have documented the impact of long working hours. The modern-day workplace, with computers, laptops, and long commutes, has brought upon us a range of stressors, such as burnout, chronic pain, insomnia, anxiety, loneliness, increased competition, and a number of other health problems. We've been in need of a more sustainable work schedule for a while now.

How to Negotiate a Four-Day Workweek

Your employer could be one of the many that still have not wound the four-day workweek into their policy. Know that you have the power to ask for it—and negotiate when possible. Often, it only takes a handful of people to drive this kind of change.

The first step is to pitch a four-day-workweek experiment to your manager. In my first job out of college, I told my boss that based on my previous experience (and the research), managing my time differently would be better for my productivity, reduce my commute, and even save costs for the company. Luckily, my manager agreed to let me try it out, and within a year, our entire team had switched to a shorter week.

If you want to have this conversation with your own boss, here are a few strategies to help you get started.

1. Track your productivity

Do you have extra vacation or flex time you can use this month? If so, before approaching your boss, experiment with taking a couple of Fridays off in the next few weeks and notice how that impacts your productivity. Make sure you have a clear and accurate way to measure your work output (and avoid simply tracking your hours).

For instance, compared with a five-day week: Were you able to meet the deadlines you set for yourself and deliver on projects? Were you able to attend all your meetings? Did you have enough time to connect with your team members in meaningful ways? Did you feel more focused, energized, or engaged one week over the other? Document your work schedule, including any obstacles you faced, as well as what worked well for you versus what didn't.

If you find that you are more satisfied at work with the shorter work, it's time to prepare for a larger conversation with your boss.

2. Think about how your decision would affect your colleagues

Whether you're an individual contributor or a manager, you're likely to work with colleagues across different functions. Requesting a four-day schedule is going to impact your teammates and their work, so think about what exactly those impacts will be.

Would you have to figure out new ways of collaborating with certain team members? Would you have to re-organize the meetings you keep each day of the week? How would your team's deliverables change if you were to move forward with this new schedule?

These are all questions you should be able to answer before approaching your boss.

You may be unsure if your coworkers even find a four-day workweek appealing. To gauge their interest, start by proposing your idea to a small group of trusted peers. Share the results of your experiment and see how they react. If their response seems favorable, you may want to encourage them to try the experiment themselves.

Bringing allies to your conversation with your boss and requesting flexible time as a group is likely to be more effective. If possible, I suggest making the ask with a group. That said, be sure your colleagues are all-in. It's better to have fewer people who are fully committed than to have more people who are not.

The final step here is to work on a proposal for an official four-day-workweek experiment that you can then present to your manager as a team. Write out the key performance indicators (KPIs) you will measure, how you will measure them, and how you plan to set boundaries at work. For example, you may propose that by working one less day a week, you expect worker productivity to increase, and customer or audience engagement to increase by 30% as a result. Your KPIs will of course vary depending on what job or field you work in.

3. Have the conversation with your manager

Once you've done your homework, you're ready to talk with your manager. As I mentioned, it will likely be more effective to approach them as a team, but either way, be mindful about how you reach out.

Set up a meeting with the intent of sharing your views. Either you or a teammate could take the lead on this. I recommend giving your boss a heads-up about the purpose of the meeting to set some expectations: Let them know that the group wants to share a proposal focused on rethinking the work schedule, and that you would be incredibly grateful for a little of their time. (Do not bring up this issue during a regular team meeting. It will catch your manager by surprise and make it harder for them to respond.)

During the conversation, put your views forth in a straightforward way. Start with something like: "Numerous other innovative companies are trying the four-day workweek to boost creativity and productivity. We'd like to work with you on an experiment for a month to see if we can make this happen. We've brainstormed a few ways to measure our results. We think this experiment will demonstrate our innovative spirit as a department to the larger company and show that we are making a real effort to adjust to this new world of work. Is this an idea you'd entertain?"

Next, share your proposal, which should include how you want the experiment to run and how you aim to measure your success as a team. Perhaps you could replicate the model you used for your own productivity tracking—spend two weeks working four days and two working five days.

Leave room for your manager to share their thoughts, concerns, and feedback during this conversation. They may have questions about the specific details, like the hard and soft boundaries you will set around your work: Will we email after hours? What will Fridays look like? What kinds of crises can the team preventatively plan for? How will this work with key stakeholders or partners outside the company who *will* be working five days?

4. Test the experiment

If you get the green light, nail down a start date. Once the experiment begins, you may find it useful to have a team meeting at the end of each week to reflect on how people are feeling and being impacted by this trial period.

Was everyone able to follow through on setting hard boundaries around their time? Were there urgent texts or emails that spilled over to day five? Has the team met or effectively worked toward the KPIs you set in your proposal? Are there some members who prefer to work five days rather than four? How has everyone's personal productivity and self-care been affected?

Share these reflections with your manager and get their feedback. When the experiment comes to an end, you should have all of the information you need to do a full evaluation and come to a consensus around how to move forward.

If your manager denies your initial proposal, don't give up. Revisit the conversation again in a few months. We are living in times of rapid change, and your boss may feel differently one week or month to the next.

If, however, you encounter a situation where your employer is not open to this discussion at all, use the moment to reflect on whether your company is a long-term fit for you and your career growth. Remember that you're not at fault for making a request.

Intelligent employers will see these shifts in our thinking and our questioning of the 9-to-5 workday as a good thing. The flexibility to control our own schedules is integral to our contributions at work. The big question is: How many employers are willing to evolve beyond what the industrialists handed us in 1926?

Whether or not your employer aligns with this changing world, I encourage you to take action and empower yourself to reclaim your time.

———————

Joe Sanok is the host of the popular podcast *The Practice of the Practice*, which is recognized as one of the top 50 podcasts worldwide, with over 100,000 downloads each month. Bestselling authors, experts and scholars, and business leaders and innovators are interviewed in the 550-plus episodes he has done over the last six years. He is originally from Traverse City, Michigan. You can learn more about his work and find additional resources by visiting his website at joesanok.com.

Getting Work Done

CHAPTER 7

How to Get More Done in Less Time

by Amantha Imber

Fun fact: A whopping 96% of people check their mobile phone within one hour of waking up in the morning (and 61% take a peek within the first five minutes).

While it may seem harmless, checking our phones as soon as we open our eyes sets us up to have a "reactive" kind of day.

Think about it.

If the first thing you do when you roll out of bed is open your email, read your texts, or listen to your voicemails, you are essentially putting yourself second. Whether good, bad, or no news awaits, you are letting other people set your mood for the day.

Adapted from "4 Ways to Get More Done in Less Time," on hbr.org, February 5, 2021.

Most of us are guilty of this, and it inevitably affects our productivity.

I spend most of my time thinking about just that: how we can be more productive in ways that feel manageable and good. Over the past three years, I've interviewed people in every field—from publishing to entertainment to the corporate world—to figure out how we can proactively structure our days to get more out of them.

Through these discussions, I've heard, time and again, that you can't let other people's priorities determine the course of your day. Rather, you must be deliberate about how you wake up, organize your time, and fit work into your schedule.

Here are four tips from highly productive people that have stuck with me—and that I hope will work for you too.

1. Align your most important work with your chronotype

Your chronotype is just a fancy way of saying "your body clock." It refers to the natural 24-hour sleep-wake cycle we all experience. Everyone has a unique chronotype, and it influences the peaks and troughs of energy we feel throughout our days.

Around 10% of people are stereotypical *larks*, who feel most energetic in the mornings. At the other end of the spectrum are the 20% who are *owls*, or people who do their best work at night. Most of us lie somewhere in middle and experience peak alertness before noon, an energy dip after lunch, and a second wind in the late afternoon.

Dan Pink, author of *When: The Scientific Secrets of Perfect Timing*, told me that paying attention to your chronotype and structuring your tasks around your energy peaks can help you get a lot more done in less time.

"On days I plan to write, I do it in the mornings, when I'm most alert," he told me. "I set myself a word count and I won't do anything until I hit it. I won't bring my phone into the office with me. I will not open up my email. Once I've hit my goal, I'm free to do other things." Pink takes full advantage of the energy he feels upon waking by using his mornings for deep, focused work—and avoiding any and all distractions.

When he has an energy dip in the mid-afternoon, he tends to stick with easier tasks. "I'll spend that time answering emails, or filing and scanning things," he said. "Then, when I get my second wind and come out of the trough around three or four o'clock, I do tasks that don't require me to be locked down and vigilant, like interviews. During this time, I feel more mentally loose, creative, and open to ideas."

As a result of sticking to this schedule, *When* was the only book Pink submitted to his publisher on time.

Pro tip

To plan your workday better, start the process of restructuring your day by determining your chronotype.[1] Broadly speaking, *larks* wake naturally at around 6 a.m. or earlier, *middle birds* wake prior to 8 a.m., and *owls* like a sleep in, but then go to bed typically after midnight. Align your energy peaks with the work that requires the most intense brainpower.

2. Plan your day the night before

A productive day doesn't just happen. It requires planning. When we write down what we intend to do—and when and where we intend to do it—we are far more likely to achieve our goals.

Google's executive productivity adviser, Laura Mae Martin, told me that she plans her day the night before. To start with, she writes down her top three priorities on the Daily Plan template she created. "Underneath the first priority, it says, 'Until this first task is finished, everything else is a distraction.' So that's my one thing I need to get done."

She then uses the template to plan her day at a micro level, hour by hour: "Even just writing down that I plan to work out between 7 a.m. and 8 a.m. makes me more likely to do that." Martin's process also includes what she refers to as "snack-sized to-dos," which are tasks she can do in between meetings, as they only require a few minutes, like making a phone call or replying to emails.

Pro tip

Take control of your day with some meticulous planning. The ideal time to do it is at the end of your workday so that whatever needs to be tackled tomorrow is still fresh in your mind.

3. Develop different rituals for different types of work

Being deliberate about where you work from is another way to add structure to your day. Consider doing what Cal Newport, Georgetown University professor and author of *Deep Work*, does, and deliberately link different locations with different types of tasks.

"When I'm trying to solve a theoretical computer science proof, the rituals I use almost always involve various walking routes around my town," Newport explained.

But when doing writing work, you'll find Newport approaching it in a completely different way. "In my house, I had a custom library table built that was reminiscent of the tables at the university library where I used to work as an undergraduate. It had brass library lamps next to the dark wood bookcases. When I sit there, writing, I have a bright light shining right down on the desk, and it's just me and my computer."

Think about the main categories of work that you do, and start to create rituals around them. The rituals might involve your physical location or the time of day you complete a certain task. For example, you may prefer clearing your inbox while sitting outside on a sunny porch, and prefer doing your Zoom calls in the quiet of your bedroom.

Pro tip

Practice these rituals for at least a couple of weeks. It takes time to get into a flow, but it will become easier and happen more quickly the more your practice. Your brain will begin to associate cues—like your physical environment and the time of day—with certain types of work.

4. Avoid being 100% booked

It's easy to assume that the most productive people are booked solid for 100% of their day. However, most of the people I've spoken to have said quite the opposite.

Darren Murph, the head of remote work at GitLab, the world's largest all-remote company, told me that being booked 100% of the time is a huge risk.

"If you have your entire day blocked with meetings, it leaves no room whatsoever for real life to happen. If your child stubs their toe, for example, and you need to address that even for eight minutes of your day, it can have a catastrophic negative impact on your mental health and on the schedules of other people," Murph said.

In addition, when you have no free time on your calendar, you leave little room to have serendipitous conversations, or moments of creativity and inspiration.

Pro tip

A fully blocked day can give you a false sense of productivity. If your calendar looks full, deliberately schedule time to do nothing. You can use this time as a buffer for things that run over or unexpected tasks that crop up during the day. Or you can even use it for planned spontaneity—times for unexpected ideas to be sparked.

Productivity isn't about how many hours you work, or how many to-dos you're able to cross off your list. It's about doing what you need in order to work in an efficient and time-effective manner. And that starts with being intentional about your day. Don't leave it to chance—use these tips to get started.

———

Amantha Imber is the founder of behavioral science consultancy Inventium and the host of *How I Work*, a podcast about the habits and rituals of the world's most successful people.

NOTE

1. "Interested in Understanding Your Chronotype?" Amantha Imber, accessed December 9, 2021, https://www.amantha.com/what-is-your-chronotype/.

CHAPTER 8

Staying Focused When You're Working from Home

by Elizabeth Grace Saunders

No commute. No drive-by meetings. No dress code. Remote working can seem like a dream—until personal obligations get in the way. These distractions are easy to ignore in an office, but at home it can be difficult to draw the line between personal and professional time.

Consider when you're working on a project and get a call from a friend. You know you need to finish your

Adapted from "How to Stay Focused When You're Working from Home," on hbr.org, September 28, 2017 (product #H03WZ4).

work, but you feel rude for not talking when you *technically* could. Or think about when you're planning your daily to-do list, but also need to decide when you'll squeeze in your personal commitments. Taking the time to put a few loads of laundry in the washer midday can seem like a quick task—until you find yourself making up that time late at night. In the end, it's never entirely clear when you're really "on" or "off."

As someone who has worked from home for 16 years, and been a time management coach for remote workers, I've seen and experienced the good, the bad, and the ugly. I've found that the most focused and effective remote workers set up boundaries for themselves so that they can actually get work done.

Here are some tips for how you can make remote work more productive and satisfying, whether it's an everyday occurrence or an occasional day away from the office.

Establish Working Hours

It may sound silly, but if you want to have a focused day of work, pretend you're not working from home. Before I became a time management coach, my schedule was chaotic. I didn't have a set time that I would be at my computer, and I would often schedule personal appointments or run errands during the day. And since my personal life didn't have boundaries, my work life didn't either. When I was home, I would feel guilty for not checking business email at all hours of the day and night. I never felt that I could truly rest.

But a big shift occurred when I set up "office hours" for working from home (for me, that was about 9 a.m. to

6 p.m. most weekdays) and clarified what was or wasn't acceptable to do during that time. I'd ask myself, "If I was in an office, would I do this task during the day?" If the answer was no, I knew I needed to do the activity before or after office hours. Household chores, errands, and spending time with friends all became activities that needed to happen before or after work. Sure, I would still field an occasional call from a friend during my lunch break, or if I had an urgent task like an emergency car repair, I'd make it happen during the day. But these were exceptions, not the rule. In setting this boundary, I not only created dedicated work time but also found that I could focus on personal items guilt-free "after hours."

Structure Your Day for Success

Maximize the effectiveness of your time at home by structuring it differently than a typical workday. For example, if you work from home only one day a week or on occasion, make it a meeting-free day. If you can't entirely avoid meetings, reserve at least half a day for focused work. Choose a time that works best for you, based on any required meetings and your energy levels.

Then define one to two key items that you want to accomplish during this time. These could be tasks that require an hour or more of uninterrupted attention, or they could be items that simply require more creative, strategic thinking than you may be able to achieve in the office environment. It's also helpful to shut down your email during this period—or at least stay away from it for an hour at a time. Alert any colleagues of times that you'll be disconnected, so they won't be surprised by a delayed response.

Set Boundaries with Others

To make your efforts stick, be clear with the people who might see your work-at-home days as simply days you're at home. Explain to friends, family, and other acquaintances that the days you're working remotely aren't opportunities for non-work-related activities. For example, if you're home with your spouse, tell them, "I'm planning on being on my computer from 8 a.m. to 5 p.m. today. I'm happy to chat at lunch, but other than that I'll be occupied." Typically, when you set expectations and stick to them (say, really stopping at 5 p.m.), people understand your limits instead of assuming you'll be available. (I also recommend having a place where you're away from anyone else who might be home, such as an office or bedroom where you can shut the door and be out of sight.)

In situations where you may have unexpected visitors, you'll need to be diplomatic. If a neighbor pops by, be open for a conversation for a few minutes, just as you would with a colleague who stops by your desk. But don't suggest they come in for a cup of coffee or have an extended discussion. Instead, use a graceful exit line like, "It was so wonderful to talk with you, but I've got some work to finish up," and then set a time to meet up after hours or on a weekend. Or, if your landlord says he'd like to stop by to do some repairs, offer a time or day that works best for you, rather than letting him take the lead.

If you do need to take on non-work-related requests during the day, set expectations for how much time you have, based on what your schedule is like in the office. For example, if your family asks you to run errands, estimate what you can do during a lunch hour, then commit only to that. For example, say, "I'm happy to pick up the dry cleaning and some milk at lunch, but I won't have time for full-scale grocery shopping until after work." Or break down errands into smaller pieces, such as, "I can drop off the car at the mechanic today, but won't get to calling about the health insurance question until tomorrow."

When you explain your limits, you don't need to do so apologetically. Lay them out factually, having the same respect for your time working from home that you would have if you were on-site. As you consistently communicate and live by these expectations, other people will begin to expect them, and you'll find yourself having more time for focused work.

Elizabeth Grace Saunders is a time management coach and the founder of Real Life E Time Coaching & Speaking. She is author of *How to Invest Your Time Like Money* and *Divine Time Management.* Find out more at www.RealLifeE.com.

CHAPTER 9

Being Mindful in an Online Working World

by Alyson Meister and Amanda Sinclair

It's no surprise that online work depletes our energy and resilience. During the Covid-19 pandemic, for example, the evidence shows that many of us worked longer hours, suffered chronic stress, and burned out at levels the world had never seen. At the same time, we were longing for and losing our social connections and sometimes experiencing profound loneliness and grief in solitude. To make remote work sustainable—to regain energy, find renewed pleasure in our work, and truly connect with

Adapted from "Staying Mindful When You're Working Remotely," on hbr.org, March 16, 2021 (product #H068HK).

colleagues and friends—we need to find ways to block out the noise in our virtual reality.

One way we can do that is by cultivating mindfulness—online.

Mindfulness is the choice we make to be present in the here and now: this moment, in this meeting, with this person or group of people. Research shows that most activities of our working lives, from an independent task to team meetings and one-on-ones, benefit from being conducted with mindfulness. By pausing, checking in with others, or starting meetings with a few moments of meditation or reflection, our stress levels drop and we feel more connected to our purpose and to others in the room. We listen better and feel happier.

But how can we be mindful in an online working world? How can we be truly present for others when we aren't physically near one another?

Online and remote working doesn't have to be a barrier to our capacity to deliver leadership presence, empathize and connect with colleagues, and build strong workplace communities. And you don't have to retreat to a mountaintop or a meditation cushion to practice mindfulness. You can do it while working from home with a few simple steps:

- Pause and notice where your thinking mind is.

- Purposefully bring your awareness to the people and context that are with you virtually.

- Suspend your narratives, agendas, judgments, and ego to offer your full online presence, evidenced through eye contact, warm and responsive facial expressions, and minimized multitasking.

You can apply these three principles of mindfulness to managing and leading online.

From Doing to Being: Offer Your Presence

Action is the hallmark of managers. It's what they're noticed for and measured on: doing, achieving, producing, organizing, controlling. New remote and hybrid working environments have thrust managers into excessive patterns of "doing." But sometimes, who and how you're *being* can be more important than your actions.

To cultivate trust and motivate and inspire others, pay attention to how you're being with them. Are you rushed or distracted? Is your mind on the next meeting or your to-do list? To enhance the quality of your leadership presence with others, take a moment to reflect on your physical and emotional state when entering a new meeting. Through your virtual presence, what energy will you convey to this set of colleagues or clients? Will you bring the tough conversation you just had with someone else into this new one? Will you offer a sense of calm and reassurance?

Someone's presence (or lack thereof) is noticeable. When a colleague is speaking, are you using the moment to check your email, send a text, or schedule a meeting? You may think that none of this shows in online working contexts. But just as in a face-to-face meeting room, virtual participants know whether and how you're truly present with them—emotions and attention can be broadcast, felt, and are contagious across virtual boundaries. Even in a big online town hall, the audience can sense if the speaker is truly with them, and the speaker knows if most of the audience is elsewhere. If you know you just can't help but look, turn off those enticing email notifications.

Lead by example when working remotely. Try to have your camera on, and ask others to do so if possible. Ensure others can feel your presence by establishing eye contact, and use your body language and posture to convey interest and empathy. If you know you just can't help but look, turn off those enticing email notifications.

It's OK to turn cameras off sometimes too: for example, if your background doesn't allow for cameras on, or during long meetings when you may need a break to stretch, stand up, or rest your eyes. We're all more comfortable seeing the cat walk across the keyboard or the toddler demand attention—it's part of life now and shows your willingness to be open and authentic. You can also still convey your engagement through active participation in the chat function.

Shifting your focus to how you're being doesn't mean that things don't get done. And none of these shifts in your awareness and attention take more than a few moments. But they do have an impact on you and on those you're working with.

From Future to Present: Be Here, Now

Managers are taught to relentlessly plan for the future. Yet always having your mind on next month's targets or next year's profits can mean you miss life today. You forgo important opportunities for connecting with and empowering others if you're in your mind, planning the next step or worrying about something that might happen.

Take a moment to step back from the busyness and view your tasks with perspective. What or who is important right now? Ask yourself: *Am I postponing life, thinking that all the good stuff will come next month or next year?* Postponing life can exacerbate unhappiness and stress. We hold out for when things will improve but don't see all the beautiful small things around us now: a fun meal with family, a morning walk or run, the sharing of a special moment or a celebration with colleagues.

Next time you're in a virtual meeting and notice your mind has wandered off, catch yourself. Bring your mind to where your body *actually* is—this present moment, right here, right now. Take a few seconds to anchor your awareness in the now by drawing on your senses. Look outside if you can, and take in any sky or trees that may be visible. Relax your shoulders and your jaw. Breathe out. These momentary connections with your physical senses are the gateways to being more present. Sharing some words of gratitude for people showing up and for what exists in the here and now can help others to pause and pay attention. They may notice they've been ruminating and can choose to tune in, not tune out. Practicing mindfulness techniques like these has been demonstrated to lift moods, foster well-being, and improve overall psychological health.

From Me to You: Enabling Connection and Community

When people are talking, where is *your* mind? Is it with them? Or are you waiting to jump in with your opinion or experience? Can you suspend your agenda and ego to hear what people on the team need? Try deepening your listening—listen without wanting to "fix" people or (perhaps silently) insisting they get over things. Deep listening is generous. Encourage the person speaking to discover and voice a way forward. They will appreciate and be empowered by it, helping them to find their own path or solution.

In our executive development work, we have found that virtual meetings can reduce barriers for people to speak and to have their voice and presence heard and felt. For example, tools like "raise hand" indicators and simultaneous chat functions enable different ways for people to offer insight and signal their contribution. Further, everyone being the same visual "size" in a virtual meeting can diminish stereotypes, hierarchies, and power differentials because certain physical and status markers are removed. As a mindful leader, be aware of who is present, and pay particular attention to inclusion. Welcome and seek people's input, especially from those who usually don't say much.

Endorsing expressions of openness and vulnerability can help cultivate a culture of appreciation and psychological safety. If you're a leader, you might offer some vulnerability about where you are right now, which will open space for others to express how they really are. Maybe you're juggling the needs of a sick child or a parent in eldercare. The circumstances of online working have sometimes meant we've had to get more real. People are tuning in from their living rooms and bedrooms. They have families, pets, and other competing needs to accommodate. We've had to take off our office masks and our constructed work identities and allow others to see us more fully. This has surely been a good thing.

Alyson Meister is a professor of leadership and organizational behavior at IMD Business School in Lausanne, Switzerland. Specializing in the development of globally oriented, adaptive, and inclusive organizations, she has worked with thousands of executives, teams, and organizations, spanning industries from professional services to industrial goods to technology. Her research has been widely published, and in 2021 she was recognized as a Thinkers50 Radar thought leader. She has recently joined the scientific advisory board for One Mind at Work, focusing on advancing mental health in the workplace. Follow her on Twitter: @alymeister.

Amanda Sinclair is an author, researcher, and teacher in leadership, change, gender, and diversity. A professorial fellow at Melbourne Business School, her books include *Leadership for the Disillusioned*, *Leading Mindfully*, and, with Christine Nixon, *Women Leading*. Amanda is also a yoga and meditation teacher, and much of her teaching and coaching focuses on introducing insights and practices from mindfulness to leading well. She recently completed her first fiction manuscript and wants her research and writing to encourage people to pause and relish life, nature, and the people around them.

CHAPTER 10

How to Leave Work at Work

by Elizabeth Grace Saunders

Some jobs have very clear lines between when you're "on" and when you're "off," while in others the lines are blurred—or potentially nonexistent. That makes not being distracted by work, especially mentally, a major challenge.

Distraction can look like sitting at dinner while your daughter tells a story about her day, but instead of hearing her you're wondering whether an email from your boss came through. It can mean the time you could have spent on sleep, exercise, or talking with your spouse is instead spent glued to your laptop. And it can lead to

Adapted from content posted on hbr.org, February 3, 2020 (product #H05E6O).

keeping your work life in order while your finances or home are a mess, because you don't take time to pay bills, plan for retirement, or tidy up.

What is possible can vary depending on your particular job, work culture, and coworkers. But in most cases, you can reduce how distracted you feel by work during times when you're not working.

As a time management coach, I've found four steps that can help. I encourage you to challenge yourself to gradually implement these changes and see how much you can leave your work at work whether you're physically leaving the office—and still checking email at home—or you're struggling to log off from your dining room.

Step 1: Define "after hours"

If you have a traditional 9-to-5 job, your hours are set for you. But if you work in an environment with flexible hours, you'll need to think through when you want to be on and off the clock. If your employer has a certain number of hours that you're expected to work each week, start by seeing how to fit those hours around your fixed personal commitments, like taking your kids to school, or extracurricular activities, like attending an exercise class you really enjoy. When do you need to start and stop to put in the proper work time?

On the other hand, if your company doesn't have a specific amount of time that you need to work—say, you freelance or have a results-only work environment—but your job still takes over almost all of your waking hours, use the reverse approach. Think through how many hours you want for activities like sleep, exercise, family, friends, cleaning, and finances. Then see how much time you need to reserve on a daily and weekly basis to fit in those personal priorities. That defines the parameters of when you want to have "off hours."

Step 2: Get mental clarity

Next, make sure you have mental clarity on what needs to get done and when you will complete it. To help you, write down the many tasks that you need to do, whether that's in a notebook, a task management app, a project management system, or your calendar. The important point is that you're not lying in bed at night trying to remember everything on your mental to-do list.

Once you have this list, plan out your work. That could mean setting aside time in your schedule to work on a report in advance, putting time in your calendar to prep for your next day's meetings, or just plotting out specific hours that you will reserve for getting your own work done versus attending meetings or responding to other people's requests. This planning reduces anxiety that something will fall through the cracks or that you'll miss a deadline.

The final part of increasing your mental clarity is to have an end-of-workday wrap-up. During this time, look over your daily to-do list and calendar to make sure that everything that absolutely had to get done—specifically, those tasks that had a hard deadline—was completed. You can also do a quick scan of your email to ensure any urgent messages are attended to before you leave the office. For some people, it works well to do this as the last thing of the day, 15 to 30 minutes before heading out.

For others, it's better to put a reminder in their calendars for an hour or two before they need to leave. This gives them a more generous time period to wrap items up.

Step 3: Communicate with your colleagues

In some job situations, you can set a definite after-hours boundary: *After 6 p.m., I'm offline.* But in other situations, the lines are much blurrier.

For those in situations where you can have a clear dividing line between work and home, I would encourage you to directly communicate that with your colleagues. For example, you might say, "I typically leave work at 6 p.m., so if you contact me after that time, you can expect to hear back from me sometime after 9 a.m. the next business day." In some cases your actions can simply set that tone. If they never hear from you between 6 p.m. and 9 a.m., that will set the expectation that you're not available.

But for others who have jobs that require more connectivity, you may want to set some guidelines to control *how* people reach you, thereby reducing unwanted interruptions. For example, you could say, "It's fine to text me during the day with questions, but after 6 p.m., please send me an email instead of a text unless the situation is truly urgent." Similarly, if you have a very flexible schedule where you take extended breaks during the day for things like going to the gym or picking your kids up after school, encourage people to reach out to you in specific ways that you establish. For instance, "There are some times during the day when I may be away from my computer. If you need a fast response, call or text me."

In these scenarios, you'll know that only the most important work will take you away from your personal or family obligations via an urgent call or text, and you can turn your attention to nonurgent work once you have the bandwidth.

Step 4: Get work done at work

It may seem obvious to say this, but I want to encourage you to give yourself permission to do work during your established work hours. For many, they perceive "real work" as something they reserve for after 5 or 6 p.m., once they've tucked their kids into bed for the night or everyone else has left the office. People have that mindset because this time can seem like the few precious hours where no one is dropping by your office, sending you Slack messages, or asking you for anything immediately. But if you want to stop feeling distracted by work at night, you need to actually do your work during the day.

Completing the actions I outlined under the mental clarity step will take you a long way in that process. Really guard your time. Set aside a few hours for project work. Block off a few minutes in your calendar to answer email. And if follow-through requires going to a place other than your office to work, do it. Make and keep meetings with yourself to knock off tasks. When you're stressed out because you haven't gotten your work done, it's exceptionally difficult—if not impossible—to not be distracted by work.

And if you must (or want to) do some work outside of your standard day, make sure that you timebox it. For example, *I will work from 8–9 p.m. tonight, then stop.* Or,

I'll put in three hours on Saturday from 1–4 p.m., but I won't think about work before or after. It's much better to designate a time and stick with it than to think about work all night or all weekend and do nothing.

As individuals, we need a mental break to do our best work, and taking time for ourselves—without the distraction of work—can help us become our best selves. I can't guarantee that thoughts about work will never cross your mind, but with these four steps, you can reduce how much you're distracted by work after hours.

Elizabeth Grace Saunders is a time management coach and the founder of Real Life E Time Coaching & Speaking. She is author of *How to Invest Your Time Like Money* and *Divine Time Management*. Find out more at www.RealLifeE.com.

Staying Connected

CHAPTER 11

Did You Get My Slack/Email/Text?

by Erica Dhawan

When we are all working from the office, we know the unwritten rules of communication. If someone has large headphones on, they are focused on work and don't want to be interrupted to gossip about the latest drama. If your team is about to have an important meeting with a client, you quickly run through last-minute questions before walking into the room.

We all learned these communication norms by observing our colleagues. But with more companies adopting a flexible way of working, and with some colleagues working different hours, on different days, from different locations, there is a need to create new rules for digital

Adapted from content posted on hbr.org, May 7, 2021 (product #H06C87).

communication. Somehow it seems that the more platforms we have at our disposal, the more complicated digital communication gets.

To understand the challenges that we all face in workplace digital communication, I did some research with Quester and surveyed almost 2,000 office workers. We found that over 70% experienced some form of unclear communication from their colleagues. The average employee wastes four hours per week on poor or confusing digital communications, which adds up to $188 billion wasted across the American economy every year, on average.

Here's an example of one organization that was struggling with this very issue. The company brought me in to assess a team's digital communication channels. The division leader wanted to know why there was so much daily dysfunction: missed deadlines, ignored emails, reports of uncomfortable chat room conversations, and a lot of peer-based passive-aggressiveness.

It didn't take me long to discover that the team in question was using its collaboration tools in every way but the right one. In team members' hands, their instant messenger had become a devious way to avoid video-call collaboration. Members were also sharing the same messages and documents across multiple collaboration tools, making it hard for anybody to know where to go for what. Finally, some members were commenting on tasks with short instant messages, without explaining if the message was an opinion or a request for action.

Eventually, the team and I created norms around the best, most proper use of every communication channel. Figure 11-1 is what we built.

FIGURE 11-1

Setting collaboration channel norms

Tool	When to use	Response time	Norms
Instant messenger (IM)	Time-sensitive, urgent messages Short and simple conversations	ASAP	Use with fewer than six people (otherwise call) Set your availability Avoid complicated questions or conversations that require visuals
Email	Provide directional, important, and timely information Ensure there's a record of your communication Direct the receiver to an online source for more information	< 24 hrs: priority dependent	Use identifiers in the subject line for urgency and response expectation Use to share attachments Avoid when immediate response is required Not for random chitchat
Video call	Use for meetings, including external ones that could benefit from visual interaction (e.g., project check-ins introductions, deck sharing)	Schedule in advance; priority dependent	Use mute if you're not talking Meeting host clarifies if video functionality is required for participation Record calls for those who miss them
Text message	Time-sensitive, urgent messages Only use if you were unable to reach the person via other channels	Within 30 minutes if between 7 a.m. and 7 p.m.; priority dependent	Use can be adjusted if it is the preferred communication for your manager Avoid texting during meetings/working sessions

Source: *Digital Body Language*, by Erica Dhawan

Using figure 11-1 as your template, set guidelines for your own team. As I discuss in my book, *Digital Body Language,* I recommend scheduling a meeting with the sole purpose of having this norm-establishing discussion. To foster an open dialogue, frame the meeting as a group brainstorm and working session. Here are a few questions to get the conversation going:

1. What's been the most collaborative experience you've had in each of these channels?

    -   IM (Microsoft Teams, Slack, Skype, etc.)

    -   Email

    -   Video calls

    -   Texting (if applicable)

2. Based on these positive experiences, what are the norms that we want to set up for each channel? (See the rightmost column in figure 11-1 for specific examples.) As you set these guidelines, think about message length, complexity, and response time.

    -   How long is too long for an IM message?

    -   Do we want to put a limit on the number of people to include in a group IM?

    -   When (if ever) is it appropriate to text someone?

    -   What is the expected response time for emails?

3. How will we stay inclusive of our remote employees and avoid potential biases?

4. Given that many of us are working asynchronously, how will we communicate when we are working while still respecting everyone's personal time?

Once you've established your team's communication norms, the hard part is then making sure they stick—people have a habit of sliding back to their old ways. Mindful of this tendency, I worked with the team to identify two or three advocates whose role was to encourage best practices within each channel and give shout-outs to those who were modeling the right behaviors.

In addition, to eliminate situations where individuals duplicated content unnecessarily across multiple channels, we rolled out the hashtag #killduplication as a response when a message is sent on the wrong channel. If someone does not adhere to the latest hybrid collaboration norms, team members are encouraged to respond with #killduplication to make it less of a callout and more of a fun reinforcement to learn the new behavior. The hashtag is now a staple in the team culture, helping to eliminate wasted time and ensure colleagues optimize the use of each digital medium.

It's essential for managers to establish norms around digital communication with their teams. Having a detailed guide will help ensure that everyone on your team is on the same page and has the same expectations—regardless of who is working from where.

Erica Dhawan is a leading expert on 21st-century team-work and collaboration. She is an award-winning key-note speaker and the author of *Digital Body Language*. Download her free guide, End Digital Burnout, at ericadhawan.com/enddigitalburnout.

CHAPTER 12

Staying Visible When Your Team Is in the Office— and You're Not

by Dorie Clark

In an all-remote work environment, everyone's in the same situation, so it's a level playing field when it comes to managing your visibility. But as companies adopt more flexible working policies, a new question emerges: If you plan to work remotely full-time or even part of the time, how can you stay visible when your in-office colleagues are likely to have far more exposure to the boss,

Adapted from "Staying Visible When Your Team Is in the Office . . . But You're WFH," on hbr.org, July 30, 2021 (product #H06GE9).

as well as access to casually transmitted information that could prove useful to their careers and promotional opportunities?

For nearly a decade, I've researched personal branding at work, and I've discovered four key strategies that can help remote workers maintain their visibility and their strong reputation, even when measured against co-workers who are putting in more face time at the office.

Overdeliver to Combat Remote Work's Negative Assumptions

It's true that the previous stigma against WFH decreased markedly during the Covid-19 pandemic, as many knowledge workers had the opportunity to try it for themselves. But it's also probable that some leaders, as they figure out the balance of remote and in-person work for their companies, will revert to their past assumptions—namely, that employees they can't directly monitor may well be goofing off. That's why it's essential for remote workers to overindex on creating perceptions of rock-solid reliability.

This may include reinforcing that you're meeting or exceeding deadlines. For instance, if your manager has asked you to write a time-sensitive report, you could just send it to them with a simple email—or you could make your contribution more noticeable by writing something like this: "Julie, as promised, I'm attaching the ABC report here. I know the official deadline is Thursday, but I wanted to send it over to you early so that we have more time to make revisions if necessary." This verbiage stops being effective if you use it too often (you don't want to come across as a brownnoser). But used sparingly, it can draw attention to your ability to deliver in clutch situations. And the short phrase "as promised" is almost always effective in reinforcing that you live up to your commitments.

Resist the Pull of Transactional Relationships

Colleagues working together in an office have plenty of organic opportunities, from elevator rides to break room encounters, to develop a low-key, ambient awareness of each other's lives (everything from where they last vacationed to what their favorite sports teams are). That information isn't essential to performing your job, of course, so it's easy to overlook its importance. But it provides a form of "social glue" that enables you to connect with colleagues beyond the purely transactional format of Zoom calls to discuss a particular project or account.

Research has shown that online negotiations are far more likely to be resolved successfully when participants share personal information with one another and thereby create a bond, rather than sticking to "just the facts" of the deal.[1] Similarly, a colleague who feels a personal connection to you is almost certainly more likely to advocate for you when you're not in the room, or volunteer to help you even when it's not convenient, as compared with someone you have a more distant relationship with.

As a remote worker, you'll have to think harder about how to engineer these connections; you can't rely on bumping into someone who invites you to lunch. You'll likely have to be the initiator, whether you decide to invite colleagues for one-on-one video chats, host a virtual networking event, or send a random instant message. But the effort is worth it, given the powerful impact of social connections on both your reputation at work and your ability to do your job successfully.

Make Yourself Physically Visible

Where geographically feasible, try to come into the office occasionally to meet with colleagues and ensure, particularly for new hires you haven't met yet, that they can "put a face to the name."

Similarly, even if your office culture permits online meetings with the video camera turned off, make a point of keeping yours on and ensuring your face is well lit, with a professional backdrop. This may seem like a minor aesthetic point, and overkill if other colleagues are keeping their cameras off. But if those colleagues are putting in more face time at the office, the people around them have far more data to use (in the form of interpersonal interactions) in forming judgments about them. If you're working from home full-time, on the other hand, this is the *only* way you're connecting with colleagues, so you need to be hypervigilant about how you're presenting yourself.

Ensure You're Easy to Work With

For obvious reasons, overextended managers appreciate employees who are willing to adjust to their schedules and work around their preferences. As a remote worker, you're never going to be as accessible as someone sitting 10 feet away, whom they can grab when a question arises or a new idea pops into their head—so you'll need to make yourself easy to work with in other ways.

For instance, it's valuable to have an explicit conversation about your manager's communication preferences. Do they find phone calls to be the most efficient way to connect? Or are they an adherent of email, Slack, or text messages? Make sure you understand how—and when—they expect to be able to reach you, how they'd prefer that you contact them, and their assumptions around response time, including during early mornings, nights, and weekends.

You'll be far more successful if you understand, and honor, their desired communication style, even if it's not your natural preference. Your goal is to minimize friction in their ability to connect with you when needed. Similarly, even if your boss hasn't requested it, it's useful for you to suggest a regular (perhaps weekly) one-on-one check-in meeting, ideally on video. That ensures you'll have at least a small amount of direct contact every week, including an opportunity to ask questions, clarify expectations, and keep your boss updated on your progress.

The risk when working from home is that your contributions fade into the background until the point when your boss and colleagues feel that you're no longer essential to the enterprise. By following these four strategies, you can stay visible and ensure that you're viewed as a valued contributor who makes a significant impact on your team's success.

Dorie Clark is a marketing strategist and keynote speaker who teaches at Duke University's Fuqua School of Business and has been named one of the top 50 business thinkers in the world by Thinkers50. Her latest book is *The Long Game: How to Be a Long-Term Thinker in a Short-Term World*. You can receive her free Long Game strategic thinking self-assessment at dorieclark.com.

NOTE

1. Don Moore et al., "Long and Short Routes to Success in Electronically Mediated Negotiations: Group Affiliations and Good Vibrations," *Organizational Behavior and Human Decision Processes* 77, no. 1 (2003): 22–43.

CHAPTER 13

Working on a Team Spread Across Time Zones

by Donna Flynn

It's 5 p.m. at my house in Nederland, Colorado, and I remember that I have a 6–7:30 p.m. team meeting. I need to plan the family dinner around it. I head to the kitchen to prep a chicken and vegetables, timing them so they will roast and rest during my meeting and we can sit down to eat as soon as I am done. In Grand Rapids, several team members will join the meeting at 8 p.m., after their dinners and evening plans. In Hong Kong, it will be 8 a.m. and Elise and Yushi will be either at the studio or still

Adapted from "Managing a Team Across 5 Time Zones," on hbr.org, June 17, 2014 (product #H00V3S).

at home, since the train commute can take a while. In San Francisco, Meike will likely call in from the Coalesse Studio. The meeting today is "no Paris" since it is 2 a.m. there and Beatriz will be sleeping.

At Steelcase, we all understand that the rhythm of a global team is not a perfect 9-to-5 melody. But understanding something can be very different from living it. My team has grown increasingly distributed across multiple time zones and regions of the world over the last couple of years, and we have learned, through experience and experimentation, a few ways to leverage the value of a global team while also minimizing the pain and disruption it can create for us as individuals. Since this is a shared experience for many multinational teams, I want to offer five global team practices we've adopted.

Share the burden of 24/7 across the team

We will never be able to change our human circadian rhythms, even though some of us may be early birds and others night owls. Time separation on a global team presents one of the biggest physical, cognitive, and emotional challenges. Despite all our "understanding" of being a global team, we used to always privilege Grand Rapids (U.S. eastern standard time) in our meeting schedule and make our Asia team members stay up late. Several months ago we started a rotating meeting schedule. Every month, each team member has one evening, one midday, and one early-morning meeting and misses one meeting that falls in the middle of their night. No team member is expected to attend a team meeting between 10 p.m. and 7 a.m.

Schedule consistent meetings to help far-flung people connect

Serendipitous encounters with colleagues around the world are still limited with our current technologies. We have learned that having consistent meetings where people can connect in both formal and informal ways is critical for fostering team cohesion. Our team has weekly meetings to provide this structure—and we make them long enough to allow for technology connection hiccups, formal sharing of project work, and catching up on vacations, travel experiences, or life stage celebrations like engagements or new babies. We are also prototyping a global "social hour" where we are all invited to bring coffee, lunch, or a cocktail—depending on where you are and what time it is—and hang out together on videoconference. Every team needs to think about what may be best for them, but you'll want more of these checkpoints than you would need for a fully colocated team.

Use as many collaboration tools as you need to—and constantly search for better ones

The tools available to distributed teams today aren't perfect. There is no one technology that does everything we need, so we use many of them for different purposes. Videoconferencing applications have come a long way and are continuously improving, but there are still challenges. Though we have a high-resolution telepresence in our offices, inevitably some team members joining from home can't connect. We have cycled through several desktop video platforms in the last few years, and

BREAKING FREE FROM A 9-TO-5 CULTURE

by Rebecca Zucker

Clarify What Needs to Be Synchronous

Distinguish which tasks and activities are better conducted synchronously. These tend to be things like project kickoff meetings to set roles, responsibilities, expectations, and deadlines, as well as client meetings (and potentially prep for these meetings). At my own leadership firm, given the limited time the partners have together, we reserve partner meetings for topics that require more in-depth discussion and debate or that require high-stakes decisions to be made. Anything that doesn't fall into these categories, such as status updates or straightforward questions on various topics, are posted on the appropriate Slack channel for others to read and respond to at their convenience.

In addition, higher-touch activities, such as conducting one-on-ones; providing others with coaching, feedback, and mentoring; and some onboarding activities should also be conducted live. To help reduce feelings of loneliness that remote work can cause, fundamental activities like team building are also important to schedule synchronously.

Rebecca Zucker is an executive coach and a founding partner at Next Step Partners, a global leadership development firm. Follow her on Twitter @rszucker.

Adapted from content posted on hbr.org, July 27, 2021 (product #H06HIP).

are constantly learning new ones, and they all have their individual quirks. We are still searching for the best videoconference platform, and telepresence is limited since we always have some team members joining from home. We've found that it takes a lot patience and flexibility to use these tools effectively. It also takes adaptability to swap out tools in the moment as needed—such as when a video connection is unstable and we have to switch to conference call because the bandwidth in Hong Kong is experiencing latency.

Pay extra attention to your colleagues who are on the phone or on video

At Steelcase, we talk a lot about the concept of "presence disparity." In meetings that bring people together via different communication channels, individual "presences" don't necessarily have the same weight in the conversation. For example, people in the same room are more likely to talk to each other and forget about the person on the video screen and the person on the speakerphone. Likewise, it's easier to enter the conversation as a distributed participant on video than on the phone because your visual presence helps get people's attention. We are consistently looking for new ways to solve for this reality of modern communications at Steelcase—and yet too often our own teams succumb to its allure by privileging those who are physically present over those who are joining from afar. The most powerful tool for this is *awareness*—remember the value that your colleagues around the world bring to the table, and honor them with consistent inclusion in the conversation. Practice eye contact with people on video, gently pause a passionate conversation in the room and ask the remote participants to chime in, or experiment with equalizing presence by having everyone call into the videoconference or conference call individually.

Invest in bringing the team together on a regular rhythm to foster team cohesion

No tool can replace being in the same room. I bring my globally dispersed team together twice a year for workshops, which have proven invaluable for renewing personal ties, building trust, and having unmediated and embodied experiences together. I have three rules for these workshops: We should build something together, we should learn something together, and we should have plenty of informal social time. The team also uses these meetings to engage in strategic discussions or decision making, since it's much more effective to reach alignment around complex issues when we are in the same room. Recently, we gathered in Paris for our spring workshop and accomplished all of those goals. We finalized our team goal for the coming fiscal year and developed our integrated team plan with clear alignment to our corporate strategy and fiscal-year priorities (we built something together). We spent an afternoon envisioning our team future through an experimental theater exercise developed at Otto Scharmer's Presencing Institute at MIT and another afternoon visiting a museum (we learned together). Finally, we ate a lot of good French food and tasted some local wines (we had informal social time). The experience of these two weeks every year spurs our team's performance for the other fifty weeks. A smart travel budget is a necessary component for a high-performing, globally integrated team. All of these different approaches add up to increasing our team's empathy for one another. This compassion fuels trust, engagement, and collaboration—and drives our business forward.

———————

Donna Flynn is vice president, global talent management at Steelcase WorkSpace Futures.

CHAPTER 14

How to Stay Connected to Your Work Friends

by Shasta Nelson

Once when I worked full-time in an office, I stopped by my favorite colleague's desk to catch up on the TV shows we had watched the night before. Later that morning, another coworker offered to get me an iced coffee (my favorite) on his trip to the local café. At lunch, I spent a few minutes talking to the person who sat next to me. Even my boss checked in to see if I wanted to walk around the block to "stretch my legs and catch up" before our last meeting.

Adapted from "How to Stay Connected to Your Work BFFs," on hbr.org, September 30, 2020.

That was back when I was actually paid to hang out with the same people five days a week, eight hours a day.

My connections with those people are what I—and probably most of us—love about work. When it comes to socializing, work is to adults what school is to kids. Our (best) work friends actually help us stay motivated and happy. And, yes, research confirms this.

I asked more than 550 professionals (ages 20 to 70) nearly 30 questions as part of a study to learn more about how people build meaningful relationships at work. Here's what I found:

- Although only 40% of the respondents "definitely" or "probably" have a best friend at work, nearly 79% of them consider a coworker to be a friend.

- Those with a best friend at work were around 30% more likely to report being "often" or "almost always" happy than those without one.

- Those without a best friend were 37% more likely to be "often" or "always" lonely.

- Those who spent their time in close proximity to their teammates were twice as likely to feel connected and energized.

Other studies show that to have a productive and (relatively) stress-free day, we need at least six hours of social interaction. People are social animals. Connecting with others minimizes our feelings of anxiety and maximizes our feelings of support.

So, even though you may be enjoying a more flexible schedule, you are likely not getting as much face time with your work friends. That can be hard. Sometimes it may feel like you're losing out on friendships—not because you don't want to stay in touch, but because you simply haven't figured out how to keep up with one another now that proximity and built-in time together are not on your side.

How do you reconnect with the colleagues you miss?

In my research, I've found that there are three principles behind any strong relationship:

- Consistency: how regularly and frequently you interact with each other determines how reliable a relationship feels.

- Vulnerability: how you get to know and feel close to each other determines how meaningful a relationship feels.

- Positivity: how many positive emotions you feel in each other's company.[1]

Each of these principles can help you define and strengthen your work friendships. Based on them, here are some ways to stay connected with your colleagues, despite being far apart.

Initiate a conversation and be consistent

The first step is to figure out *how* you can connect with colleagues virtually—even those who haven't reached out to you yet. When people are distant, it's too easy to think,

"Well, it seems like they don't miss me or care about our friendship." But that is most likely not true. It's more likely that your friend feels the same way as you or is going through something that's hard for them to share. Try not to take their silence personally, and be willing to initiate a conversation.

If this person really matters to you, pick up your phone and text, "I miss seeing you! We clearly can't rely on proximity and spontaneity now to stay in touch . . . any chance you'd be up for scheduling some time to catch up?"

Then, figure out new rituals to stay connected. Or, recreate an existing ritual. If you always ate lunch with a certain colleague, maybe you can now do that virtually once a week.

Remember that you can't connect if you don't make time, and you can't make time if you never initiate.

Pro tip

Before you end your chat, be intentional about connecting again. Say, "Thank you so much for taking the time today. This was fun! I think we should speak again soon—perhaps in two weeks? What do you think?"

It's OK to be vulnerable

During the conversation, be candid. My definition of friendship is any relationship where both people feel seen in a safe and satisfying way. That signals vulnerability: All of us want to be seen. We don't want to simply update each other with the facts of our lives; we want to feel known and understood.

In practice, this kind of connection is built by asking questions and sharing your emotions. For example, good questions to ask are: What are you proud of? What's giving you hope these days? What's draining your energy? What's annoying you lately? What's motivating you? What helps you feel focused?

Create a safe space to focus on not just the pleasant or positive emotions but also the difficult feelings. We all experience things differently, so it's important to be curious about what other people are going through. When we can share our struggles without judgment, we can show up for each other, no matter what's going on in our lives.

Pro tip

Ask each other, "What's one thing bringing you joy this week and one thing causing stress?" or, "Where do you feel like you're winning and where could you use some support?"

Make the other person feel validated

When we share something about ourselves, what we crave the most is acceptance. No one wants to reach out and be candid if they're going to be judged for it. We connect with each other hoping to feel more loved, so the most important thing we can do is respond to vulnerability with validation. Make the other person feel good about sharing their time with you.

When you talk to a friend, focus simply on mirroring back what you hear them expressing. We often make the mistake of giving advice and trying to cheer the other person up, when all they want us to do is make them feel like we "get" them. If your friend is excited, say, "That does sound fun!" or if they're going through something difficult, "That must be really disappointing."

The more the conversation leaves you both feeling good about yourselves, the more you will both want to stay in touch.

It's likely that your views, values, or beliefs will change over time—and that may be true for your friend as well. Remember that it's OK for your work friendships to evolve. The most important thing, though, is that you both end the conversation feeling accepted.

Pro tip

Affirm them. Express your appreciation or encouragement. Say, "I always love connecting with you. And I'm cheering you on as you finish that big project. They're lucky to have you managing that."

When a conversation leaves you and your friend feeling good about the shared time (positivity), you are more likely to make time with each other (consistency), and that will leave you feeling like you know each other better (vulnerability).

I know syncing up calendars and planning schedules doesn't sound too exciting, and it'd be better if these relationships felt more organic. But trust that showing up for your work friends (even virtually) can help you feel closer to them both now and whenever you're together in person.

Shasta Nelson is a friendship expert, keynote speaker, and a leading voice on loneliness and creating healthy relationships. She works with organizations to improve their culture and employee engagement. Her research is found in her three books, including her newest one, *The Business of Friendship: Making the Most of the Relationships Where We Spend Most of Our Time.* She has been a featured TEDx speaker, and her expertise has been highlighted such places as the *New York Times*, the *HBR IdeaCast* podcast, and *The Steve Harvey Show*. For more information, visit www.ShastaNelson.com.

NOTE

1. Shasta Nelson, "Frientimacy: The 3 Requirements of All Healthy Friendships," filmed November 2017 at La Sierra University, Riverside, California, TEDx video, 16:23.

CHAPTER 15

New to the Team? Here's How to Build Trust (Remotely)

by Ruchi Sinha

Trust isn't easy to build. It develops slowly, typically after you and another person have spent some time interacting and assessing each other's character.

If all goes well and trust builds, you start to feel psychologically safe and can form a stable belief about one another. But remote and flexible work makes all of this difficult to do.

Adapted from content posted on hbr.org, March 23, 2021.

Many of us are interacting through our screens and working on hybrid teams with people located in various areas of the world, who are online at different times of the day, and who we're not likely to get solid face-to-face time with. We lack the luxury of regularly observing our peers in person, making it harder to gauge their intentions, values, and characters (and vice versa).

This is a challenge. In any kind of work environment, you need trust for all kinds of reasons. Without it, you may not feel comfortable bringing your full self to work. You and your teammates may struggle to support one another or openly share ideas and opinions, leading to damaging miscommunications, decreased productivity, and a fear of taking risks that could help you learn and grow in your career.

As an academic, I have explored trust in many different contexts, including how it is rebuilt in the aftermath of conflict, how leaders build trust in teams, and how the emotions we express during negotiations impact it. Through my own work and through reading the literature on trust, I've learned that the fundamentals of how we judge the trustworthiness of others remain the same across relationships. There are ways to build and sustain trust if you know how to send and receive the right signals.

Here are three of the most readable indicators of trust. The good news is you can display them whether you are at the office or remote and can encourage them on your team.

Competence

Competence is your ability to do something efficiently and successfully. When others perceive you as competent, they believe that you have the skills and knowledge to do what you say you will. This allows them to perceive you as dependable, reliable, and predictable—all of which are essential drivers of trust. Some things you can do to signal your competence include the following.

Being organized

Before team meetings, do your homework and study the agenda. To show that you are prepared, show up with a list of questions, research, or solutions that may be of interest to the stakeholders involved in the project. Your peers will see that you are a motivated and organized team player.

Showing reliability and consistency

If you've told one team member no about meeting a certain deadline, don't switch to a yes when another member asks. If you have critical feedback on a project, don't tell one coworker and hide your concerns from another. People inherently associate consistency and commitment with dependability. Treat everyone fairly, and make sure your behaviors match your values.

Being thoughtful about what you promise

Don't commit to things that you don't have the time or motivation to deliver on. Also, avoid overpromising and underdelivering (like saying yes to a deadline that is two days away when you know it will realistically take you a week to get things done). When talking to teammates, avoid making generic statements of support ("Yeah, good idea, we should do something about that"). Instead, offer actionable ways in which you can support them when you like their ideas ("Hey, I love that idea—I am happy to help you write out an action plan next week"). Likewise, if you don't agree with an idea, be honest and don't give inauthentic support.

Being predictable and dependable

Remove the mystery around your actions by explaining your motives, values, and criteria. For example, when you suggest ideas to your colleagues, you can say, "Here is what I think we should do: Let's focus on doing X. I am suggesting this because I have considered the following facts: A, B, and C. Here are my assumptions and rationale for why these facts have led me to pick X over other options. I am open to feedback and would love you to weigh in on the best path forward."

Benevolence

Benevolence is the quality of being well-meaning and the degree to which you have others' interests at heart. Colleagues will grow to trust you to the extent they believe you care about their interests and will go beyond your self-needs to cater to the team's needs. Some things you can do to signal your benevolence include the following.

Identifying similarities

People will be more open to your ideas if they feel your values overlap with theirs. Identify the topics and goals you and your teammates share by engaging them in genuine conversations. For example, when someone shares a thing or two about their life at the start of a meeting, try to relate to them in some way by sharing something from your own. When someone asks how you're doing, take it as an opportunity to engage authentically. Be honest about the challenges and struggles you are facing—and ask questions back. Finally, when you talk about your ideas, link them to your values. This will give others a chance to make deeper connections with you. The more your peers understand where you are coming from, the more likely they will be to support you.

Showing kindness and compassion

Small gestures make a big difference. During informal catch-ups or conversations on Slack or IM, take the time to ask your teammates how they are feeling, and show genuine interest. People will likely see you as someone who cares about the needs of others, and as a result believe you are more trustworthy. For example, you could pitch in to help a colleague who is struggling with a family emergency or shout out your colleague's work at the next team meeting. When others see you as someone who shows kindness and compassion, they are more likely to interpret what you say in a positive light.

Showing restraint

Be careful about the words you choose. During meetings, make sure your comments are not dismissive. Avoid scoffing and eye-rolls no matter how disinterested you may be. Don't dominate the conversation; instead, make sure everyone gets a chance to speak. Avoid gossip. If a teammate has shared a personal struggle with you, it is not your place to share it with others. You need to care about privacy at work. Be mindful of managing personal and professional boundaries so that you can be trusted with sensitive information.

Integrity

Integrity is how you adhere to strong moral principles and how honest you are. Integrity is hard to judge and critical for building trust. A lot of behaviors at work can be perceived as strategic actions, leaving people unsure of whether they are coming from someone's underlying values or are merely a façade. Thus, the more opportunities you have to articulate your values explicitly and to allow team members to see your values in action, the more likely they will be to have faith in you and invest their trust in you. Some ways to demonstrate integrity include the following.

Showing loyalty

Find ways to signal your support of and allegiance to your team members. Endorse the reputation of your team to external parties, defend the group's vision and mission, and act in the interest of the team's goals rather than your personal goals. If your manager praises you for a presentation you just delivered, and three colleagues helped you put it together, give credit where it's due. Instead of saying, "Thank you, I worked hard on it," you can say, "Thank you. I'd like to acknowledge all the help I received from X, Y, and Z."

Listening

When you consider your teammate's perspectives before you make decisions, you show through your actions that you are reflective and deliberate, as opposed to impulsive. For example, if you find yourself in a disagreement, instead of retaliating with a counterargument, first take the time to listen to your colleague. Try to understand their side of the argument. Ask clarifying questions and then make your point. You could say, "The way I see it, you mean X." This shows that you listened to their points and that you want to understand them before you react—and not just "win" the argument for the sake of winning.

Showing "citizenship"

Go beyond your duties to personally do better than what is expected of you and to help others achieve excellence. For example, you could take the initiative to act in prosocial ways by offering to teach skills to colleagues that can improve their performance at work. Are you a pro at Excel? Lead a mini master class for your peers.

Successful teams are made of successful teamwork, and for that, trust is key. Show your coworkers that you're worthy of their trust by displaying the traits highlighted above. Be consistent, and look for consistency in the actions of your peers. That is how they will develop stable beliefs about your character, and how you can measure whether or not it's worth investing your time and trust in them.

———————————

Ruchi Sinha is an associate professor of management at the University of South Australia Business School. Her research explores how voice, trust, conflict, and power dynamics influence work and negotiation outcomes.

Making the Most of Meetings

CHAPTER 16

What It Takes to Run a Great Hybrid Meeting

by Bob Frisch and Cary Greene

New flexible work models are bringing dramatic changes in how we meet—a hybrid mix of in-person attendees and remote meeting participants. As Satya Nadella, Microsoft's CEO put it, "We want to ensure those joining remotely are always first-class participants."

Hybrid meetings are vastly more complex than meeting in person or virtually. They are easy to do poorly and hard to do well—remote participants are only one slip-up away from losing that first-class status.

Adapted from content posted on hbr.org, June 3, 2021 (product #H06DY4).

Drawing from our combined half-century of experience designing and facilitating meetings for executive teams and boards, we've assembled eight best practices to help make your hybrid meetings more effective:

Up your audio game

Although remote participants need to see who is talking and what's taking place in the meeting room, great audio is actually more critical. Yet while a lot of attention is paid to the visual aspects of meetings, audio is often overlooked until the last minute. Pre-Covid, we often heard remote participants say, "I'm sorry, can you get a little closer to the speakerphone and repeat what you just said?" Now, they expect to hear everything clearly— just as they can on Zoom.

To avoid a last-minute scramble caused by poor audio, make sure the room is equipped with enough high-quality microphones so remote participants can hear. If you're in a hotel or other temporary meeting space and multiple microphones aren't a viable option, consider supplementing your audio input by having in-person attendees pass around a handheld microphone before speaking.

Explore a technology boost

The pandemic accelerated the use and evolution of videoconference technology to enable virtual meetings from PCs, tablets, and phones. As providers invest heavily to better enable hybrid meetings, new features are being introduced to improve face-to-face communication among in-person and remote attendees.

For example, Zoom's Smart Gallery uses artificial intelligence to detect individual faces in a shared room and pull them into panes on the screen so remote participants can see them in the now-familiar gallery view. Microsoft is developing new types of meeting rooms optimized for the hybrid experience. You should investigate what technology upgrades might be accessible to help make your team's experience more immersive and authentic.

Consider video from remote participants' perspective

As you design the meeting, continually ask yourself: What do remote participants need to see in order to fully engage? They should be able to see the faces of in-room attendees, presentations shared, physical documents handed out, and content created during the meeting on whiteboards or flip charts.

It is tempting to just ask the in-person attendees to open their laptops and join a Zoom meeting (on mute) so that remote participants can see everyone's faces and documents can be easily shared. Clients frequently suggest this type of "in-room virtual meeting." However, if the folks gathering in the room spend the meeting on their computers, they might as well have stayed in their homes or offices. The last thing you want is for them to crouch over—and be distracted by—their individual laptops all day for the sake of the remote participants.

Especially in cases where cutting-edge video technology is unaffordable or unavailable, a little ingenuity can go a long way toward creating a high-quality video experience for everyone.

For example, for a two-day off-site at a Florida hotel with 10 in-person attendees and two remote participants (one in Zurich and one in Los Angeles), we attached three webcams to laptops and used a fourth laptop to share what was on the main screen (usually a PowerPoint). We mounted two of the webcams on tripods, which faced the in-room attendees so remote participants could see who was speaking. We moved the third camera around to show a close-up view of presenters, flip charts, and wall charts throughout the session as needed. The four laptops joined the two used by our remote executives for a total of six separate Zoom "participants" in the single Zoom meeting.

Post-meeting feedback confirmed that this setup allowed the remote participants to feel like they were an integral part of the meeting rather than distant observers.

Make remote participants full-sized

Another way to give remote participants equal stature is to give them greater presence in the room. In addition to the main screen in the center, set up two additional large monitors—one on each side of the room—showing "life-size" panes of the remote participants for the duration of the meeting.

We find these large images help in-person attendees accept remote colleagues as full participants and provide a constant reminder to include them in the conversation. Similarly, if possible, the voices of remote participants should emanate from the same monitors as their faces—

ceiling speakers tend to reinforce the artificiality of the situation.

Test the technology in advance

Nothing kills a meeting's momentum like waiting to fix a glitch in the audio or video. Prior to an important meeting, test the audiovisual setup—both in-room and for the remote attendees. Schedule a 10-to-15-minute one-on-one dry run to get remote participants comfortable with what they will see and hear during the meeting, as well as to review any software features they'll likely be asked to use. It's well worth the brief time required.

Design meetings for all attendees

Review each activity or exercise that will happen during the meeting, focusing specifically on how remote participants will engage. Consider what tools and techniques, digital or otherwise, can be used to maximize their interaction with the in-room attendees.

For example, if you need to poll the group, use a phone-based survey tool to collect everyone's input in real time. This puts remote participants on equal footing, versus relying on a show of hands or verbal feedback. To capture meeting notes, use an online whiteboard (or focus a remote camera on a flip chart) so everyone can see what's being written as it happens.

Similarly, if the meeting design calls for in-room attendees to put dots or Post-its on a wall chart, use a webcam to allow remote participants to read their peers' responses before placing their own, just as they could if they were physically present.

If the meeting design calls for putting people in breakout groups, it may seem like the easiest solution is to include all the remote participants in a single group. But while simpler, this sends them the wrong message by reinforcing their physical absence. It's likely worth the extra logistical and technical effort to integrate remote participants across several breakout groups to accentuate their equal status.

Provide strong facilitation

Managing a hybrid meeting is harder than when the whole group is in person or on Zoom together. One person—a staff member, an outsider, or a meeting participant—should be assigned to guide the conversation and keep it on track.

Despite the effort you may put into meeting design and logistics, it remains far too easy for in-person attendees to dominate the discussion. A facilitator should draw the remote participants in, keep them engaged, and ensure their voices are heard, not interrupted or talked over. At times, the facilitator may need to call on in-room or remote participants to ensure equal participation.

Give each remote participant an "in-room avatar"

There may be times when remote participants need a physical presence in the room. It could be as simple as a camera view being blocked. Maybe a microphone isn't working, or an attendee needs to be reminded to speak up. A Post-it may need placement on a wall chart, or a poker chip placed on a table as part of a resource allocation exercise.

For these situations, each remote participant should have what we call an "in-room avatar"—a staff person (or fellow participant) who can be their physical presence in the meeting room as required. Whether via text, chat, or phone, they should have a private line of communication constantly available throughout the meeting. Remote participants tell us that having confidential access to a single point of contact goes a long way toward removing a sense of isolation or distance from those in the room itself. Consider how embarrassing it is for a remote participant to have to ask, "Fred, can you please speak up? I can't hear you" every time Fred speaks. It's much better to have another person come up to Fred during a break and discreetly say, "Fred, please speak louder. It's really hard for Natasha to hear you from Zurich."

By leveraging technology and tools, being thoughtful in meeting design, and providing strong facilitation, we can create hybrid meetings where all participants—whether in the room or an ocean away—feel engaged, valued, and equal.

———————

Bob Frisch is the founding partner of the Strategic Off-sites Group. He is the author or coauthor of four *Harvard Business Review* articles, including "Off-Sites That Work" (June 2006) and "When Teams Can't Decide"

(November 2008), in addition to 20 articles for hbr.org. Bob also wrote the bestselling *Who's in the Room?* and coauthored *Simple Sabotage*. His work is included in eight HBR collections, including *HBR's Must Reads on Teams*.

Cary Greene is the managing partner of the Strategic Offsites Group. An expert in strategic alignment and facilitation, he is coauthor of *Simple Sabotage*, the *Harvard Business Review* article "Leadership Summits That Work" (March 2015), and over 15 articles for hbr.org. His work is featured in seven HBR collections.

CHAPTER 17

When Do We Actually Need to Meet in Person?

by Rae Ringel

Three days in the office, two working from home? Or two weeks in the office, then two at home (or some other, more alluring remote locale)? Everyone in all the time?

These are some of the options leaders are considering as they grapple with what work should look like. Some of these arrangements are landing uneasily. At Apple, for example, employees pushed back against a policy requiring them to be in the office three days a week, describing a "disconnect between how the executive team thinks

---

Adapted from content posted on hbr.org, July 26, 2021 (product #H06GZ0).

about remote/location-flexible work and the lived experiences of many of Apple's employees."

To get beyond this stressful push and pull, we need to reframe the conversation and focus on what we're actually trying to achieve rather than where, precisely, we'll be sitting when we achieve it. This involves examining the precise nature of the tasks in front of us, our specific objectives, and the weight we attach to factors such as efficiency, effectiveness, camaraderie, and mental health. Once we determine which parts of our work should be done in person, which should be virtual, and which can benefit from a mix, we can design toward that ideal.

As Priya Parker notes in *The Art of Gathering: How We Meet and Why It Matters*, "Gatherings consume our days and help determine the kind of world we live in." And so, to ensure that we're mindful of how we spend our time, it's critical that we reimagine a cornerstone of the modern workplace: how we meet.

As you plot out your team's work plan, here are six questions you should be asking.

Should this be a meeting?

Your and your colleague's time is valuable—and it's draining when the vast majority of our time seems to be spent in meetings.

Think very carefully about whether time spent meeting might be better spent thinking, writing, or engaging in other projects. Less is more: The fewer meetings we have, the more the ones we do have will count. It all comes down to purpose. Ask yourself: *Why are we meeting?* Be sure the answer makes sense. Do you really need to meet? Prioritize asynchronous work, and use meetings to be creative and do something together, rather than simply to share information.

For example, meetings for team members to provide progress reports—where every individual has their segment but is relatively passive the rest of the time—may not be necessary. Here, the goal of sharing progress may be accomplished more efficiently in writing. On the other hand, brainstorming sessions, where people are building off of one another's ideas, benefit from the dynamics of a gathering.

Are my meeting goals relationship-based or task-based?

Task-based goals might include updating a board, briefing constituents, or planning an event. These goals can often be accomplished in a virtual meeting (if a meeting is deemed necessary at all).

Relationship-based goals, which involve strengthening or repairing connections among team members, are *usually* accomplished most effectively in person. People should be given difficult feedback face to face. Challenging group conversations should also take place in person, where destructive and distracting parallel side chats can't overshadow the central discussion.

Why do I say "usually"? Because I've participated in some meaningful virtual meetings where participants bonded and opened up in ways that I doubt they would have in person. For some people, the screen creates a sense of psychological safety, and with it the freedom to share views and take risks. Sometimes, relationship-based goals may require an unexpected pop-up meeting. In these cases, it's often preferable to handle the matter immediately, over Zoom, rather than a few days later in person. An example of this might be a quick meeting to clear up a potentially damaging misunderstanding or, on the positive side, to celebrate an unanticipated win by a team member.

How complex are my objectives?

Sometimes complexity is a more helpful framework for determining what form a meeting should take. This includes emotional complexity and the level of interdependence that certain decisions or outcomes may require.

Figure 17–1 plots out goals according to their relative level of complexity. You may notice some correlation between relationship-based goals and complexity, but the overlap is not complete. Meetings to determine capital allocations or significant investments, for example, may land squarely in task-based territory. But if these discussions involve navigating interpersonal and other complexities, or carefully balancing competing priorities, they might best be navigated in person.

At the same time, relationship-based goals can be relatively simple. One of my favorite success stories is my experience running a large real estate firm's Zoom holiday party. For the firm, Bernstein Management Corporation, this gathering is an opportunity to celebrate and acknowledge employees—as straightforward a goal as there is.

"If you asked me a year ago whether I would have considered hosting a virtual holiday party, I would have

FIGURE 17-1

Do you need to meet in person?

Use this tool to gauge a goal's relative complexity.

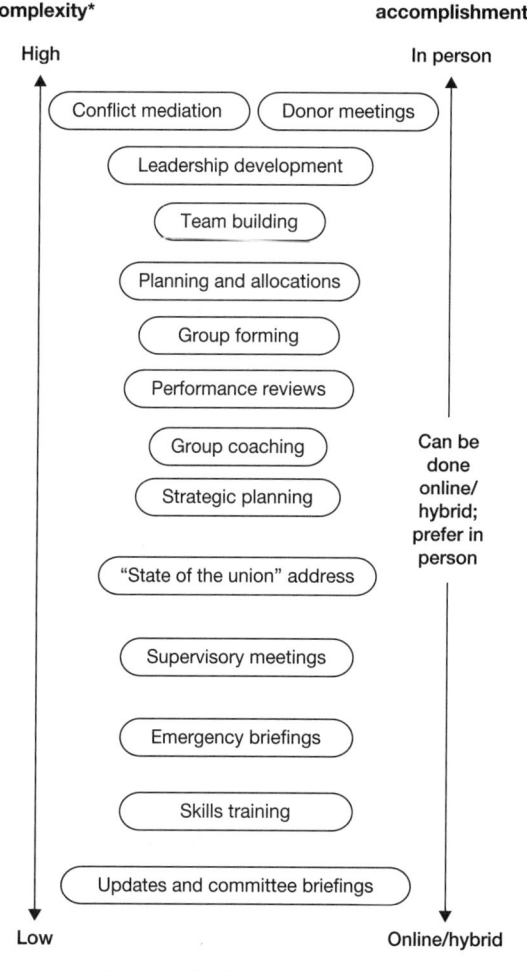

given an unequivocal 'no' and questioned the judgment of the person asking," the firm's CEO, Joshua Bernstein, told me. "But in many ways, it worked out better. Every single participant was focused on the same conversation. There wasn't a bad seat in the house. Almost everyone expressed their surprise at how enjoyable the program was, and that element of surprise and newness ended up being part of the success."

Could my meeting take an entirely different shape or form?

There's the in-person meeting room, there's Zoom, and there's hybrid. But there's also a world of possibilities that don't fall into any of those categories. Now that we have so many more tools at our disposal, are there other ways that information could be imparted so that it's absorbed more effectively?

One of my clients has replaced her monthly all-hands staff meeting with a prerecorded video that staffers can watch or listen to on their own time—perhaps while they go for a jog or prepare dinner. If they miss something, they can rewind. This approach honors different types of learners; some of us actually retain information better when we're able to multitask. Companies that go this route can ask employees to watch the video by a certain date, then offer optional Q&A follow-up sessions on a platform like Slack or even WhatsApp.

When I work with clients virtually, we often assign a scribe to each breakout room. The scribe takes notes on the conversation in a Google Doc. When we come back together, everyone takes a "gallery walk," spending several minutes scrolling through the Google Doc, reviewing what the other groups came up with, and annotating ideas they like. This circumvents a phenomenon known as "death by report back": when representatives from each group drone on about the ins and outs of their conversations while others spend the whole time figuring out what they're going to say when it's finally their turn to speak.

What type of meeting will be most inclusive?

A few years ago, I believed that the cohort-based Executive Certificate in Facilitation program that I run at Georgetown University needed to happen in person, once a month, for four months in a row. The participating senior managers and executives would fly in from all over the world for three days at a time. The deep interpersonal connections forged among participants were critical to our success—after all, we were teaching them how to help other groups form trusting bonds. Although I've been facilitating remote workshops for over a decade, I doubted that this particular program could pivot.

I was wrong. In fact, one of the most significant advantages of the virtual format we were forced to use during the pandemic is that it's been more inclusive. People from overseas or the West Coast have no jet lag to contend with. Those whose organizations are willing to cover their tuition but not their flights or hotels no longer face those financial obstacles. We had more mothers with young children participating than ever before.

This isn't to say that we didn't experience a real sense of loss from our inability to be together in person. But our program has many objectives and encompasses a broad swath of different activities or tasks. Some of them, like those that have a tactical focus on design and team development, can be extremely effective online.

Moving forward, we're planning to hold two of our four modules in person and two virtually. This is a different and, yes, more inclusive way of doing hybrid: Instead of having some people participate in person and some on a screen, everyone will be on equal footing—maximizing each person's contribution and the benefits of each medium.

Does my facilitator have the skills and tech setup to pull off a hybrid gathering?

As companies figure out post-pandemic hybrid work, there's a strong temptation to hold in-person meetings with a remote option for those who need it. This can be an excellent solution when done well, allowing everyone to show up from the place where they feel most comfortable. But there are special skills involved in facilitating a hybrid meeting. Done incorrectly, you can end up sidelining and even alienating remote participants.

Skilled hybrid facilitators know how to make Zoom participants feel like full participants. They establish clear protocols for everyone to offer input. They make direct eye contact not only with those in the room but also with the camera.

Technology and preparation are key. One of my colleagues showed up at a New York City hotel, energized for the fully in-person gathering she thought she was about to lead. Only when she arrived did she realize that a handful of participants would be joining online. She tried her best to improvise, but she'd designed a physically active program that involved moving around the room. It didn't immediately translate to a virtual environment—at least not with the technology available. By the end of the day, the in-person participants were fully engaged, but every single virtual participant's camera was off.

Until those running your meetings hone their skills in the art of hybrid facilitation and have the technology to support them, consider holding an entirely virtual meeting, even if many participants are Zooming in from the office.

Given all that we overcame during the pandemic, it would be a shame if we didn't take advantage of every single hard-earned pearl of wisdom around work, life, and the nexus of the two. Let's harness our new perspectives on time, technology, and togetherness to rethink how we work—and specifically, how we gather.

Rae Ringel is the president of the Ringel Group, a leadership development consultancy specializing in facilitation, coaching, and training. She is a faculty member at Georgetown University's Institute for Transformational Leadership and founder of the Executive Certificate in Facilitation program at Georgetown's School of Continuing Studies.

CHAPTER 18

How to Nail a Hybrid Presentation

by Sarah Gershman and Rae Ringel

We recently spoke to a CEO who was feeling anxious about public speaking in the hybrid office. "When I give presentations and everyone is on Zoom, it's simple," he told us. "What happens when some people are in the office and others are working from home?"

His anxiety makes sense. While Zoom presentations are far from ideal, at least the audience is on an equal playing field in terms of screen space. Hybrid presentations, on the other hand, run the risk of putting remote

Adapted from content posted on hbr.org, May 5, 2021 (product #H06C2R).

participants at a serious disadvantage. A major reason has to do with the energy created when we are physically together—and the energy that is missing when we're not. We derive our shared energy in part from the nonverbal cues that happen when we are together in the room. The knowing glances, the facial expressions, and the personal eye contact are all part of what makes conversation flow more naturally. This is tangibly absent online, and the lack of shared energy among remote participants can be enervating (hence one of the factors of Zoom fatigue).

Corporate leaders desiring to make hybrid presentations more inclusive, energetic, and successful can look to the classroom for guidance. We have worked with a number of teachers and educators who wanted to improve their on-screen speaking skills and presence. As some kids returned to school in 2021, we saw remarkable teachers master the challenge of teaching effectively to hybrid classrooms.

We recently had the privilege of witnessing one of them in action. This seventh-grade teacher from Bethesda, Maryland, was teaching poetry to a hybrid class. We were immediately struck by his energy. His body was in constant motion, and his eyes seamlessly moved from the screen to the faces in the room. He also encouraged the kids to move—asking for raised hands or having the remote students stand up to read. Even more importantly, he assigned small working groups where remote and on-screen kids worked together. Despite being hybrid, the class was one.

Below are seven strategies for presenters and meeting leaders to more effectively engage everyone in their hybrid audience:

Focus on the positive

Rather than getting bogged down in the liabilities of the hybrid meeting, focus on the value each person can bring. Ask yourself both how the remote and in-person participants can benefit from hearing your presentation and how the entire experience could be enriched by having a hybrid audience. A positive mindset will help you make each person essential to the presentation. Moreover, that mindset is contagious. The presenter sets the tone for the entire experience. If the presenter believes and expresses excitement about the hybrid experience, this will positively influence the experience of the audience.

Require cameras to be on

In hybrid meetings, it is more important than ever that remote participants turn their cameras on in order to show their full presence. It is also critical that the presenter be able to engage visually with the entire audience, not just with those in the room.

To level the playing field even further, consider asking in-person participants to bring their laptops and turn their cameras on, keeping themselves on mute when not talking. It can also be helpful to have a screen in front of the room so that remote participants can be seen by everyone.

Make direct eye contact

Begin your presentation by first looking deliberately and directly at the camera. This sends the whole group a message that the people on Zoom are critical. Try to focus on the camera as if you were making contact with one person. Then throughout the presentation, continue to switch between looking at individuals in the room and returning your focus to the camera.

Move around to include everyone

When your presentation begins, move toward the camera to help remote participants feel connected to what is happening in the room. As you continue speaking, move purposefully toward the people in the room and then back again toward the camera. But be sure to keep the camera frame in mind—you don't want to venture too far out of the shot. This back-and-forth movement communicates greater inclusivity and makes participants both in and out of the room feel more connected to each other.

Also consider spotlighting: If someone in the room is speaking, lift the camera (laptop) and move it closer to the speaker (if they didn't bring their own). This reminds the people in the room that their remote colleagues are part of the meeting.

Emotionally engage remote participants

The hybrid model need not be a passive experience for those who are dialing in. It is critical to help them feel heard and seen. Greet virtual participants personally at the beginning of the session, and continue to address and engage them throughout the presentation. This is easier said than done. Presenters may have the best of intentions, but their attention is naturally drawn to people in the room. Designate specific times in the presentation to speak directly to the remote participants, and build into the content messages that are directed specifically toward individuals dialing in.

Foster hybrid collaboration

When dividing a larger presentation into smaller groups, the temptation is to put the in-person and remote people in separate groups. But this reinforces the notion that the two are separate rather than working together. Instead, try mixing it up. Have virtual and in-person participants work together.

Keep it short

Zoom has forced us to waste less time in presentations. Resist the temptation to speak for longer, and keep hybrid presentations as brief and efficient as possible. Try to time the meeting based on the energy levels of the remote participants. In the end, everyone will appreciate this.

One of the potential advantages of hybrid presentations is that everyone participates from their preferred location. The seventh-grade teacher told us that this has created greater equity in his classroom and that his class has been enriched by helping each student effectively wherever they are. This mindset is inspiring—both for his students and for business leaders. As we move into this next era of hybrid presentations, let's follow his example and strive to create an inclusive and energizing environment for each person in the audience.

Sarah Gershman is president of Green Room Speakers, a communications firm based in Washington, DC. She is a professor at the McDonough School of Business at Georgetown University, where she teaches public speaking to students from around the globe.

Rae Ringel is the president of the Ringel Group, a leadership development consultancy specializing in facilitation, coaching, and training. She is a faculty member at Georgetown University's Institute for Transformational Leadership and founder of the Executive Certificate in Facilitation program at Georgetown's School of Continuing Studies.

Managing Your Flexible Team

CHAPTER 19

Setting Flexible Schedules with Your Team—Fairly

by Joan C. Williams and Marina Multhaup

Bias against parents—and especially mothers—has been well documented. We call it the "maternal wall," and we've been studying it for years, researching how women who have always been successful at work sometimes find their competence questioned when they take maternity leave or ask for a flexible work schedule. We know now that this bias can affect fathers, too, when they seek even modest accommodations for caregiving. For example, a

Adapted from "How Managers Can Be Fair About Flexibility for Parents and Non-Parents Alike," on hbr.org, April 27, 2018 (product #H04AWW).

consultant in one study reported that he was harassed for taking two weeks of paternity leave—but applauded for taking a *three*-week vacation to an exotic locale. Parents, studies consistently show, face extra scrutiny.

But while the data is clear that parents are more likely to face bias at work, sometimes we also hear about a different problem: People *without* children find that their managers are more understanding of working parents' need for flexibility, while expecting childless or unmarried staff to pick up the slack because they "have no life." Indeed, research has found that women without children work the longest hours of any group.

How can managers set and enforce flexibility policies that are fair to everyone?

Simple answer: If you give people time off work to take care of their sick kid, you should give people time off work to run a marathon. If you give people time off work because the nanny didn't show up again, you should give people time off work because their grandmother is sick.

Though people's reasons for needing flexibility at work may differ, the principles for managing that flexibility on your team are the same.

Here are some guidelines that managers can follow to be fair to parents and nonparents alike:

In general, more-flexible schedules work better for everyone

Flexible hours benefit both parents and nonparents, but in different ways. For parents with very young children, their work schedule can be tied to the baby's sleep schedule. Parents with older kids may need to work around inflexible school or activity schedules. This helps parents be more productive with the time they have, and helps them balance their work and lives easier.

Nonparents also use flexible working hours to be more productive. Some people do their best work 7–9 a.m., while others hit their stride at 10 a.m. Workers with long commutes might try to shift their schedules to spend less time sitting in traffic, or work from home on certain days. Some people may have clients who are in different time zones, and it might make more sense for them to be online when those key accounts are most active.

What kinds of flexibility are feasible will depend on the workplace and the job. Obviously, a cashier cannot telecommute and a trial lawyer can't get home like clock-work every day at 3 p.m. But a cashier can job share, and a lawyer can telecommute or take chunks of time off once the case has settled. Given the broad array of flexible work options, from flex time (control over when you work) to remote work to job sharing (where two people seamlessly split a single job), managers can typically offer a variety of options to accommodate different workers' needs.

If you have a work-from-home policy, it should be reason-neutral

It's generally not a good idea to have to judge different people's reasons for working from home. This leads to uncomfortable territory: Does a sick baby trump a dying grandparent? Instead, when people work from home, just have them say, "I'm working from home." Don't make people explain why.

Exceptions might be when there is a reason for an employee to be in the office (like an in-person meeting) but something comes up at the last minute, or if a particular employee has shown that they can't meet their deadlines when they're working remotely. In those cases, a manager may need more transparency with their employee about what's going on.

Ensure that employees can actually use your flexible work policy

Don't tell your employees that they can take advantage of your flexible policy and then expect them to be in the office from 9 a.m. to 6 p.m. every day. Research by Deborah Rhode found that, in the legal profession, there is consistently a "huge gap between what [part-time] policies say on paper and what people feel free to use." One of us (Joan) has been studying this phenomenon for years, specifically in a 2013 article with Mary Blair-Loy and Jennifer Berdahl titled "The Flexibility Stigma: Work Devotion vs. Family Devotion." The article reported that while most workplaces allowed their employees some flexibility in working hours, the usage rates by employees were very low. The reason is because the use of flexibility policies was shown to result in negative work consequences for employees, such as wage penalties, lower performance evaluations, and fewer promotions.

Offer your employees flexible working hours, and then let them take advantage of the policy. Make sure you're not signaling that employees should actually be working "normal" hours—either through subtle means ("Oh, you're leaving already? Must be nice!") or through more direct consequences (like poor performance evaluations).

Set clear boundaries and procedures for being in touch

Flexible schedules have many upsides, but they can also have downsides. They can make managers nervous: *What if I really need to get in touch with my team and I can't? What if a work emergency happens?* They can also make employees feel like they need to be "always on" and constantly checking email. To deal with this, managers have to put a system in place for when employees need to be immediately responsive.

Establish clear boundaries and procedures so employees know when they are expected to be available and when it's OK for them to work their preferred hours. Make sure everyone is aware of, and signs on to, the rules.

For example, say your employee works from 8 a.m. to 4 p.m. but you prefer to work from 10 a.m. to 6 p.m. You could tell the employee that when you email them after they are done working, they are not expected to reply to it until the next day, unless you text them with something urgent. This will give both of you peace of mind: The employee can sign off and enjoy their life without having to worry that they are missing important work updates from you, and you can shoot off emails to your employee and cross things off your to-do list without worrying about bugging them when they're off work.

This is also a good policy to use for weekends. Telling employees that they don't need to respond to weekend emails unless they are specifically called can give your employees much-needed time to rest and also reassure you that if something urgent comes up, you can get ahold of them.

Establish trust with your employees and then trust them

When you allow your employees to manage their own schedules to best suit their strengths and lives, and when you work a schedule that fits your life, sometimes you don't work side by side every day. How do you ensure that people are working when they say they are working, that they're not skiving off work and responsibilities, that they aren't making up excuses or fake doctor's appointments?

Bottom line, you can't. And you shouldn't try to. One of the easiest ways for a comfortable workplace to become toxic is if the culture becomes one of bosses trying to trap people in lies, checking up on them unexpectedly, or generally not trusting them. There needs to be trust established between managers and employees and between coworkers for a workplace to function. Think about it this way: Even if your employee is sitting eight feet away from you, are you looking at their screen all day? Are you monitoring their every movement? No. But physical proximity can make us feel like we have a handle on what someone is doing. Spending time and energy trying to monitor what your employee is working on every second of the day isn't going to help anybody.

Our recommendation is to build trust with your employees from the beginning, and then trust them. If you feel you can't trust your employees to work out of your sight, that's a performance problem. Treat it like one.

Measure outcomes, not process

"OK, I trust my employees, but I still need to know what they're doing!"

We get it. Our advice is to measure employees by the work that they produce, rather than the manner in which they produce it.

It's time to move away from rewarding the 80-hours-a-week employee just because he puts in the most face time at the office. This continued dedication to the "ideal worker" stereotype disadvantages parents and non-parents alike, and puts emphasis on a nonessential work function. Who cares who spends the most time at their desk? Maybe that person is just woefully inefficient. What you should be asking is: Who does the best work? Who gets the most done? Whose projects are the most impeccable?

Save your scrutiny for employees' work products, not their whereabouts. This will help avoid toxic climates and will redirect employees' energy away from looking busy and toward doing their actual jobs.

Policies, policies, policies

You can manage your employees perfectly, but if your workplace doesn't have policies in place to support them, you are opening a hornet's nest. Important policies to have in your workplace:

- Paid parental leave (for all parents!)

- Paid sick days

- Paid personal days

- Paid bereavement days

- Disability leave

But don't let your supportive policies die in the employee handbook. Encourage your employees to take advantage of them.

In our office, people's start times vary from 8 a.m. to 11 a.m., and their end times vary from 4 p.m. to "when the baby wakes up." If babies are sick, parents' hours that day are "when the baby is sleeping," and when people have doctor's appointments, or have to wait around all day for their cable provider, or have to be offline for an hour to deal with a family situation, we work around it. With a little bit of communication, offices can allow everyone to adjust their hours to accommodate their employees' strengths, schedules, and lives.

––––––––––––

Joan C. Williams is a distinguished professor of law, Hastings Foundation chair, and founding director of the Center for WorkLife Law at the University of California, Hastings College of the Law. An expert in the field of social inequality, Williams is the author of 12 books, including *White Working Class: Overcoming Class Cluelessness in America* and *Bias Interrupted: Creating Inclusion for Real and for Good.* She is widely known for "bias interrupters"—an evidence-based, metrics-driven approach to eradicating implicit bias in the workplace. The website www.biasinterrupters.org, which has open-sourced tool kits for organizations and individuals, has been accessed 225,000 times in countries around the world.

Marina Multhaup is a former research and policy fellow for the Center for WorkLife Law at the University of California, Hastings College of the Law.

CHAPTER 20

The Downside of Flex Time

by Maura Thomas

Remote and hybrid work naturally leads to flex time. Employees with small children might be getting the majority of their work done at night after the kids are in bed. Others are working early and hoping to quit early. Still others are starting late and working late.

If everyone on your team is working different hours, you may be getting emails and messages at all hours of the day, night, or weekend—which can quickly create an expectation of an "always-on" environment. That might be necessary in some industries, but certainly not in every industry and not for everyone in any industry. But once this kind of culture takes root in your company, it

Adapted from content posted on hbr.org, May 14, 2020 (product #H05MER).

becomes difficult, if not impossible, to reset later. And always-on isn't sustainable. It increases pressure and quickly turns your company into an unpleasant place to work. It might cause even the most dedicated employees to consider other offers.

So how can you accommodate your employees' needs while still protecting your culture and your team's work-life balance? The key is to embrace and encourage flex time while also defining clear communication hours (for example, 8 a.m. to 6 p.m.). Outside of those hours, employees should be encouraged to change their settings to "Do Not Disturb" and to use the "schedule send" feature of their email client so that messages only get delivered during communication hours.

If any correspondence must happen outside of the set communication hours, such as for urgent or time-sensitive issues, make them phone or text only. This way people can comfortably close down all other communication channels, like email, Slack, and instant messenger. The act of having to call or text someone is usually enough to give the sender pause, so they think, "Do I really need this person now, or can the communication wait?" This allows everyone on your team to work whenever is appropriate for them but not feel like they have to work all the time to accommodate everyone else's schedule.

Here's how to improve the odds of success when implementing this policy:

Address the problem head-on

First, explicitly acknowledge the problem and emphasize the importance of downtime. This can be done in a "virtual town hall," which is a useful practice to keep everyone connected if your team is remote. These can be live or recorded messages from the CEO and senior leadership. I recommend making these leadership communications on a regular basis, and repeating the importance of downtime frequently for reinforcement. The message can be something like this: "We believe that downtime is important, and we recommend that you track the hours you spend working, and limit those to roughly 40 hours a week. Depending on your role, there may be times when more hours are required, but we expect and encourage you to balance busier times with intermittently lighter schedules."

It may be tempting to refrain from giving this implicit instruction, especially if your organization is dealing with a particularly busy or stressful period. But it will have a positive impact on your culture in the long term.

Provide guidelines for communication channels

Second, establish clear guidelines about which communication channel should be used in which situation. You should continue to practice and enforce these guidelines no matter when or where your team is working. For example, email should never be used in the case of urgent or time-sensitive communication. This treats email as a "synchronous" communication channel, and it can never be that. No one is capable of responding to, or monitoring every message in real time, and to attempt it is an exercise in futility and a sure path to stress, overload, and, eventually, burnout.

FIGURE 20-1

Communication guidelines

Type of communication	During communication hours	Outside of communication hours
Email	Routine requests, information sharing	Hold or use scheduled send
Team communication tools (Slack, Teams, etc.)	Project-related communication, socializing	Everyone set to Do Not Disturb
Phone, video calls	Relationship building, sensitive or complex topics	Time-sensitive or urgent only
Text message	Time-sensitive or urgent only	Time-sensitive or urgent only

Source: Maura Thomas

If email is ever used to communicate urgent and time-sensitive communication, you'll force your team to have to check every new message as it arrives, which is every few minutes for most people. This not only prevents downtime but also prevents your team from applying themselves to any of their important work in a thoughtful, undistracted way. I bet everyone on your team has work that requires more than a few minutes of sustained attention!

These communication guidelines should take the established "communication hours" into consideration. Use figure 20-1 an example to get you started. You should ensure you have a complete inventory of all the ways your team uses to communicate both internally and externally, and adjust your guidelines accordingly.

Use technology to your advantage

Consider technology solutions to help reinforce your desired behavior, such as programming the corporate server so that even if emails are sent outside of communication hours, they aren't delivered until the designated times. Check if your team collaboration tools have "global settings," so everyone can automatically be set to "Do Not Disturb" mode outside of the designated communication hours.

Model the desired behavior

And finally, leaders must model the behavior, or else it will never work. Anyone in the organization who manages others should follow the guidelines themselves, and also reward and discourage behaviors accordingly. For example, saying, "Thanks for being so responsive" to someone who answers an email outside of the defined communication hours sends a mixed message and will undermine the guidelines. Any "policy" that isn't followed by leadership isn't really a policy at all. And if leaders don't follow a policy, it erodes the trust, and therefore the culture, in an organization, because then you end up with "the official policy" and "the way everyone *actually* behaves."

When businesses adopt flexible working policies, it's easy for unintended results to erode company culture. If specific attention isn't given to the characteristics and consequences of the new reality, those unintended results will have detrimental effects that could last a long time. It's not too late to implement policies that will benefit your team's work-life balance while also protecting your organization's culture.

Maura Thomas is an award-winning international speaker and trainer on individual and corporate productivity, attention management, and work-life balance. She is a TEDx speaker, the founder of Regain Your Time, and the author of several books, including the Empowered Productivity series. She frequently appears in major business outlets and was named a top leadership speaker for 2018 in *Inc.* magazine. You can assess your attention management skills at www.maurathomas.com/ assessment. Follow her on Twitter @mnthomas.

CHAPTER 21

What Psychological Safety Looks Like in a Hybrid Workplace

by Amy C. Edmondson and Mark Mortensen

Psychological safety—the belief that one can speak up without risk of punishment or humiliation—has been well established as a critical driver of high-quality decision making, healthy group dynamics and interpersonal relationships, greater innovation, and more effective

---

Adapted from content posted on hbr.org, April 19, 2021 (product #H06AWX).

execution in organizations. Simple as psychological safety may be to understand, Amy's work has shown how hard it is to establish and maintain this kind of safety even in the most straightforward, factual, and critical contexts. For example, these contexts may include ensuring that operating room staff speak up to avoid a wrong-side surgery or that a CEO is corrected before sharing inaccurate data in a public meeting. (Both are real-life psychological safety failure examples reported in interviews.) Unfortunately, remote and hybrid working makes psychological safety anything but straightforward.

When it comes to psychological safety, managers have traditionally focused on enabling candor and dissent with respect to work content. The problem is, as the boundary between work and life becomes increasingly blurry, managers must make staffing, scheduling, and coordination decisions that take into account employees' personal circumstances—a categorically different domain.

For one employee, the decision of when to work from home may be driven by a need to spend time with a widowed parent or to help a child struggling at school. For another, it may be influenced by undisclosed health issues or a nonwork passion, as was the case with a young professional who trained as an Olympic-level athlete on the side. It's worth noting that we've heard from employees who feel marginalized, penalized, or excluded from this dialogue around work-life balance because they're single or have no children, often being told they're lucky they don't have to deal with those challenges. Having psychologically safe discussions around work-life balance issues is challenging because these topics are more likely to touch on deep-seated aspects of employees' identity, values, and choices. This makes these topics both more personal and riskier from legal and ethical standpoints with respect to bias.

We Can't Just Keep Doing What We're Doing

In the past, we've approached "work" and "nonwork" discussions as separable, allowing managers to keep the latter off the table. However, many managers have found that previously off-limits topics—like childcare, health-risk comfort levels, or challenges faced by spouses or other family members—are increasingly required for joint (manager and employee) decisions about how to structure and schedule hybrid work.

And with the shift to a higher proportion of WFH and flexible work, this will not be changing anytime soon. Organizations that don't update their approach going forward will find themselves trying to optimize extremely complicated scheduling and coordination challenges with incomplete—if not incorrect—information. Keep in mind that hybrid working arrangements present a parallel increase in managerial complexity; managers face the same workflow coordination challenges they've dealt with in the past, now with the added challenge of coordinating among people who may not be present at predictable times.

Strategies for Managers

Let's start with the fact that the reasons managers have avoided seeking personal details remain just as relevant and critical today as they've always been. Sharing personal information carries real and significant risks, given legal restrictions related to asking personal questions, the potential for bias, and a desire to respect employee privacy. The solution thus cannot be to demand greater disclosure of personal details. Instead, managers must create an environment that encourages employees to share aspects of their personal situations that are relevant to their work scheduling or location and/or to trust employees to make the right choices for themselves and their families, balanced against the needs of their teams. Management's responsibility is to expand the domain of which work-life issues are safe to raise. Psychological safety is needed today to enable productive conversations in new, challenging (and potentially fraught) territory.

Obviously, simply saying "just trust me" won't work. Instead, we suggest a series of five steps to create a culture of psychological safety that extends beyond the work content to include broader aspects of employees' experiences.

Step 1: Set the scene

Trite as it sounds, the first step is having a discussion with your team to help them recognize not only their challenges but yours as well. The objective of this discussion is to share ownership of the problem.

We suggest framing this as a need for the group to problem solve to develop new ways to work effectively. Clarify what's at stake. Employees must understand that getting the work done (for customers, for the mission, for their careers) matters just as much as it always has, but that it won't be done exactly as it was in the past—

they'll need to play a (creative and responsible) role in that. As a group, you and your employees must come to recognize that everyone must be clear and transparent about the needs of the work and of the team, and jointly own responsibility for succeeding, despite the many hurdles that lie ahead.

Step 2: Lead the way

Words are cheap, and when it comes to psychological safety, there are far too many stories of managers who demand candor of their employees—particularly around mistakes or other potentially embarrassing topics—without demonstrating it themselves or protecting it when people do share.

The best way to show you're serious is to expose your own vulnerability by sharing your WFH/hybrid work personal challenges and constraints. Remember, managers have to go first in taking these kinds of risks. Be vulnerable and humble about not having a clear plan, and be open about how you're thinking about managing your own challenges. If you're not willing to be candid with your employees, why should you expect them to be candid with you?

Step 3: Take baby steps

Don't expect your employees to share personal and risky challenges right away. It takes time to build trust, and even if you have a healthy culture of psychological safety established around work, remember that this is a new domain, and speaking up about buggy code is different from sharing struggles at home.

Start by making small disclosures yourself, and then make sure to welcome others' disclosures to help your employees build confidence that sharing is not penalized.

Step 4: Share positive examples

Don't assume that your employees will immediately have access to all the information you have on supporting the benefits of sharing these challenges and needs.

Put your marketing hat on, and market psychological safety by sharing your conviction that increased transparency is happening and is helping the team design new arrangements that serve both individual needs and organizational goals. The goal here isn't to share information that was disclosed to you privately, but rather to explain that disclosure has allowed you to collaboratively come up with solutions that were better not just for the team but also for individual employees. This needs to be done with tact and skill to avoid creating pressure to conform—the goal here is to provide employees with the evidence they need to buy in voluntarily.

Step 5: Be a watchdog

Most people recognize that psychological safety takes time to build but mere moments to destroy. The default is for people to hold back, to fail to share even their most relevant thoughts at work if they're not sure they'll be well received. When they do take the risk of speaking up and get shot down, they—and everyone else—will be less likely to speak up next time.

As a team leader, you need to be vigilant and push back when you notice employees making seemingly innocent comments to one another like "We want to see more of you" or "We could really use you," which may leave employees feeling they're letting their teammates down by not being physically in the office. This is a really hard thing to do and requires skill. The idea isn't to become thought police or to punish those who genuinely do miss their WFH colleagues or need their help. Rather, it's to help employees frame these remarks in a more positive and understanding way—for example, "I miss your thoughtful perspective and understand you face constraints. Let us know if there is any way we can help." Be open about your intentions to be inclusive and helpful so that people don't see requests for their presence as a rebuke. At the same time, be ready to firmly censure those who inappropriately take advantage of shared personal information.

It's important that managers view (and discuss) these conversations as a work in progress. As with all group dynamics, they're emergent processes that develop and shift over time. This is a first step; the journey ahead comes without a road map and will have to be navigated iteratively. You may overstep and need to correct, but it's better to err on the side of trying and testing the waters than to assume topics are off limits. View this as a learning or problem-solving undertaking that may never reach a steady state. The more you maintain that perspective—rather than declaring victory and moving on—the more successful you and your team will be at developing and maintaining true, expanded psychological safety.

———————

Amy C. Edmondson is the Novartis Professor of Leadership and Management at Harvard Business School. She is the author of *The Fearless Organization*.

Mark Mortensen is an associate professor of organizational behavior at INSEAD. He researches, teaches, and consults on issues of collaboration, organizational design and new ways of working, and leadership.

CHAPTER 22

Giving Feedback When You're Not Face-to-Face

by Therese Huston

Delivering constructive feedback is nerve-racking in the best of times—most managers don't *want* to crush their employees' spirits. These tough conversations are even harder to have when there is a change in venue from in-person to remote that removes the nuance that can help soften the blow of bad news.

Negativity bias shapes how people hear feedback. As Roy Baumeister and John Tierney explain in their book *The Power of Bad,* this bias is the "universal

Adapted from "Giving Critical Feedback Is Even Harder Remotely," on hbr.org, January 26, 2021 (product #H064FT).

tendency for negative events and emotions to affect us more strongly than positive ones." In other words, we ruminate over criticism and brush past praise.

That bias can be a challenge in any feedback conversation—it causes employees to be even more likely to focus on the negative in your message. If you say, "I need you to redo that report," they might hear, "Your work is really slipping," or worse yet, "I'm not sure you belong in this job." You're trying to help them improve, but they think you're judging them, and harshly.

Managers I've interviewed note that when they're giving feedback in person, they can adjust the context to communicate the severity of the news. One midlevel manager at a tech company with an open office plan used to pull employees into a focus room when he wanted a private feedback conversation. He'd pick a room with comfy, colorful chairs and a low coffee table if he wanted the environment to feel relaxed and casual, and he'd pick a conference room with chairs around a big formal table if he wanted to communicate a more serious tone. With his employees now working at home, he can't control the setting in that way.

Many managers now find themselves in this position, no longer able to rely on those nonverbal cues when having tough conversations. And since remote and hybrid work are the new normal, knowing how to deliver constructive feedback virtually is critical. Taking a few steps to be more strategic about delivering it can help mitigate negativity bias, and prevent a digital venue from distorting how your employees receive your message.

Start by asking questions

Begin your constructive feedback conversation by asking the other person about their perspective. You might ask, "What did you think of that report?" or even simpler, "How did that go?" You want to learn about their experience and what they think of their work—maybe they felt rushed and wished they'd had one more day. It will be easier to raise your concern if they've already voiced it.

What if they say they thought it went well and don't voice any concerns? You might be dealing with an unaware underperformer. If you observed the problem directly, you can say, "I ask because I noticed X," and if you didn't observe the problem yourself, try, "I ask because I heard X." In either case, you're hoping the employee is willing to brainstorm ways to handle the situation differently in the future. Be clear that they're being evaluated on their results, not their effort.

Offer appreciation before you offer criticism

In their research, Leslie John, Alison Wood Brooks, and Jaewon Yoon at Harvard Business School have found that individuals are more receptive to constructive criticism if they're first told what specifically they did well. Your goal here isn't a hand-waving, "You do good work." Instead, make it as concrete as the concern you're about to raise—for example, "It's clear you have a mastery of the data." If there isn't much you can praise about the work, praise their willingness to keep improving.

State your good intentions

John has also found that explicitly stating your good intentions goes a long way toward improving how the other person will take bad news. Try, "I'm in your corner," or "I know you're trying to improve your writing, and I want to help you get there," or even "I want to be able to use this report as a model for the rest of the team."

Clarify and contrast

Helene Lollis, the CEO of Pathbuilders, a firm that develops woman leaders, finds that contrasting statements can bring clarity. After you've raised your concern or suggestion, follow it with, "What I mean is X. What I don't mean is Y." For instance, "What I *am* saying is that I'm concerned you don't have the bandwidth right now. What I am *not* saying is that you lack the ability. I know this would be easy for you under other circumstances." You can thus preemptively address any negative spins that the other person might entertain.

Have the other person state their key takeaways

Save time at the end of the conversation to ask, "What are your top three takeaways?" It may feel redundant, but you'll learn whether the person is taking a negative nosedive, and if so, you can reframe the message. Sandy Anuras, VP of global marketing technology at Expedia Group, observes that when you're giving feedback remotely, it's far too easy for the other person to end a call more abruptly than they ever would in person. If they urgently need to get off the call, ask them to email you by the end of the day with their three takeaways. It's better to correct any misunderstandings in the moment, but doing so later that day is better than letting the person ruminate overnight or over the weekend.

While delivering negative feedback remotely can cause employees to take constructive criticism even harder than usual, delivering it with clarity and sensitivity will help them focus on the reality of your message, even when you're not face to face.

Therese Huston is the author of three books, including *Let's Talk: Make Effective Feedback Your Superpower.* She was the founding director of the Center for Excellence in Teaching and Learning at Seattle University, and she talks and consults on how to give and solicit better feedback at work. Learn more at www.theresehuston.com.

CHAPTER 23

Tips for Managing an Underperformer

by Liz Kislik

Flexible and remote work arrangements are here to stay. As the manager of a remote team, you can't afford to ignore underperformance from remote workers, whether they're temporarily at home, working in local branch offices, or half a world away.

Although you might assume that managing an underperformer in a remote environment would be more challenging (who wants to have a series of difficult

---

Adapted from "5 Tips for Managing an Underperformer—Remotely," on hbr.org, July 22, 2021 (product #H05QUZ).

conversations over Zoom?), there's actually an upside. You may actually be *more* effective in handling the situation because you have to plan and structure your interactions, rather than catching up in the hallway or waiting for them to stop by when you're in the office. Here are five things you can do to help remote underperformers improve their game.

Revisit your expectations

Take the opportunity to reconsider what you want most from the employee and why you feel you're not getting it. Start by reviewing your recent directives and whether your communications about what's expected have been clear and consistent from the beginning. This is something you do with underperformers in any context, but when you don't see the employee in person, it's even more important to ask yourself whether your statements have been ambiguous. Part of this process is separating out whether your dissatisfaction is with their work products or with the way they deliver.

If their style or approach is the problem, check to see if you're expecting them to work the way you do. If that's the case, let go of those expectations and dispassionately assess their real strengths and capacities for contributing to the team's work. When one of the senior executives I work with came to terms with the fact that he didn't care for one of his subordinates, it turned out that the remote relationship worked better because he could pay more attention to her output and the praise he heard about her from other leaders, and less attention to his own biased reactions.

If you suspect the underperformer's difficulties come from insufficient experience, specific skill deficits, or a lack of business or organizational acumen, consider whether they need training or could partner with a more experienced colleague. This may be more challenging in a remote environment, but don't let the problem fester—take action to provide the support they need.

Learn more about them

Even if the underperformer has been on your team for a while, it's important to ask about their goals and what they care about, since these things change as circumstances evolve. Plus, you don't have the benefit of casual, in-person contact to pick up details about family, hobbies, or past work successes. Then, modify your management approach to match their needs. For example, you might learn that they miss working side by side with colleagues and would perform better if they were assigned to projects that involved more regular interaction.

If you're not familiar with their remote setup and schedule, ask. Some team members may prefer strict deadlines to structure their often-interrupted workdays; others may benefit from more flexible deadlines to help them deal with the additional pressures of working from home. Take their home obligations like schooling time or eldercare into account, according them the same respect you would regular work meetings.

Level with them and be specific

You may not be in the same room, but providing feedback is still a requirement. Many people who aren't doing well have a vague feeling that something is wrong, but don't really know which of their behaviors aren't working. For example, telling a team leader that they need to "be a better listener" doesn't help them understand specifically what they need to do differently. It's much more helpful to explain that when they turn away during videoconferences or change the subject while team members are speaking, the team loses trust and confidence in them. The feedback gives them the opportunity to actively practice modifying those behaviors.

Help them learn how to improve their own performance

As much as possible, use questions to encourage them to self-diagnose and to project into their future: "How will this experience set you up to do better next time?" I often ask coaching clients, "Why do you think I'm asking you this?" to encourage them to reach their own conclusions, rather than telling them what I have observed, which doesn't trigger the same kind of "aha." Doing this will help you avoid micromanaging, which is a significant temptation when you're trying to be extremely clear about expectations.

Stay in close contact

Keep in mind that a remote underperformer can't just drop in to check on things or "take your temperature." It's on you as their manager to stay in regular touch and to keep them in the loop. Don't assume that no news is good news. After you've given an employee candid feedback and they don't hear from you, they can start to worry that you're ignoring them because you've written them off, and their performance can deteriorate further. Schedule regular meetings to talk about their progress. When a VP learned that one of her reports thought she was "ghosting" him, we came up with a consistent schedule of one full update and two quick touch-base updates each week for a few months until the relationship was on stronger footing.

If you've asked them to keep you up to date on their progress, make clear how you want them to do that. If they tend to use email, but you're awash in email and respond better to texts or Slack messages, tell them that. And don't rely only on video meetings, where the lack of true eye contact can make it seem like you're getting nonverbal clues when you're not. If you're concerned that you're not getting a good read on your team member's state of mind, plan to have at least some of your interactions by phone, and listen carefully. The tone of their voice may give you more clues about what needs intervention.

It's not easy to work with a remote employee who isn't performing well, particularly when you can't sit down together and have a conversation. But using specific, road-tested techniques to help them improve will strengthen not only their performance but their relationship with you as well.

Liz Kislik helps organizations from the *Fortune* 500 to national nonprofits and family-run businesses solve their thorniest problems. She has taught at NYU and

Hofstra University, and gave a popular TEDx talk, "Why There's So Much Conflict at Work and What You Can Do to Fix It." You can receive her free guide, How to Resolve Interpersonal Conflicts in the Workplace, at www.lizkis lik.com/resolve-conflict.

Index

Notes

Notes

Notes

Notes

Notes

Notes

Notes

Notes

Notes

Smart advice and inspiration from a source you trust.

If you enjoyed this book and want more comprehensive guidance on essential professional skills, turn to the HBR Guides Boxed Set. Packed with the practical advice you need to succeed, this seven-volume collection provides smart answers to your most pressing work challenges, from writing more effective emails and delivering persuasive presentations to setting priorities and managing up and across.

Harvard Business Review Guides

Available in paperback or ebook format. Plus, find downloadable tools and templates to help you get started.

- Better Business Writing
- Building Your Business Case
- Buying a Small Business
- Coaching Employees
- Delivering Effective Feedback
- Finance Basics for Managers
- Getting the Mentoring You Need
- Getting the Right Work Done

- Leading Teams
- Making Every Meeting Matter
- Managing Stress at Work
- Managing Up and Across
- Negotiating
- Office Politics
- Persuasive Presentations
- Project Management